T0360485

"Increasing evidence of food poverty and food insecurity experienced by people in wealthy countries is of major concern. In response, the expansion of emergency charitable food aid provision similarly evidences that the issue is being ignored by government. In this wonderful new book, Smith and Thompson work to systematically examine the UK's food environment, showing clear associations between food deserts, food poverty and mental and physical poor health outcomes. As Smith and Thompson offer a methodological framework, this book is essential reading for anyone with an interest in understanding the socio-political and geographical drivers of food poverty, and the inescapable links between food waste, food charity and poor health outcomes."

**Dr Dave Beck**, Lecturer of Social Policy,
University of Salford, UK.

# Food Deserts and Food Insecurity in the UK

This book examines the social inequalities relating to food insecurity in the UK, as well as drawing parallels with the US.

Access to food in the UK, and especially access to healthy food, is a constant source of worry for many in this wealthy country. Crises, such as the COVID-19 pandemic, have coincided with a steep rise in the cost of living, meaning food insecurity has become a reality for many more households. Providing a thorough background to two key concepts, food deserts and food insecurity, the book documents the transition from area-based framings of food resources, to approaches which focus on household food poverty and the rise of food banks. The book invites researchers to acknowledge and explore the ever changing range of place-based factors that shape experiences of food insecurity: from transport and employment to rural isolation and local politics. By proposing a new framework for food insecurity research and by drawing on real-world examples, this book will support academic and applied researchers as they work to understand and mitigate the impacts of food insecurity in local communities.

This book will be of great interest to students and scholars of food and nutrition security, public health, and sociology. It will also appeal to food policy professionals and policymakers who are working to address social inequalities and improve access to healthy and nutritious food for all.

**Dianna Smith** is an Associate Professor in the School of Geography and Environmental Science at the University of Southampton, UK.

**Claire Thompson** is a Senior Research Fellow in the Department of Health and Social Work at the University of Hertfordshire, UK.

# Routledge Focus on Environment and Sustainability

**Phyto and Microbial Remediation of Heavy Metals and Radionuclides in the Environment**
An Eco-Friendly Solution for Detoxifying Soils
*Rym Salah-Tazdaït and Djaber Tazdaït*

**Water Governance in Bolivia**
Cochabamba since the Water War
*Nasya Sara Razavi*

**Indigenous Identity, Human Rights, and the Environment in Myanmar**
Local Engagement with Global Rights Discourses
*Jonathan Liljeblad*

**Participatory Design and Social Transformation**
Images and Narratives of Crisis and Change
*John A. Bruce*

**Collaborating for Climate Equity**
Researcher–Practitioner Partnerships in the Americas
*Edited by Vivek Shandas and Dana Hellman*

**Food Deserts and Food Insecurity in the UK**
Exploring Social Inequality
*Dianna Smith and Claire Thompson*

**Ecohydrology-Based Landscape Restoration**
Theory and Practice
*Mulugeta Dadi Belete*

For more information about this series, please visit: www.routledge.com/Routledge-Focus-on-Environment-and-Sustainability/book-series/RFES

# Food Deserts and Food Insecurity in the UK

## Exploring Social Inequality

## Dianna Smith and Claire Thompson

Routledge
Taylor & Francis Group
LONDON AND NEW YORK

earthscan
from Routledge

First published 2023
by Routledge
4 Park Square, Milton Park, Abingdon, Oxon OX14 4RN

and by Routledge
605 Third Avenue, New York, NY 10158

*Routledge is an imprint of the Taylor & Francis Group, an informa business*

*British Library Cataloguing-in-Publication Data*
A catalogue record for this book is available from the British Library

*Library of Congress Cataloging-in-Publication Data*
A catalog record has been requested for this book

ISBN: 978-1-032-02675-6 (hbk)
ISBN: 978-1-032-02677-0 (pbk)
ISBN: 978-1-003-18456-0 (ebk)

DOI: 10.4324/9781003184560

Typeset in Times New Roman
by Deanta Global Publishing Services, Chennai, India

# Contents

# About the authors

**Dr Dianna Smith** is an Associate Professor in the School of Geography and Environmental Science at the University of Southampton. She has several years of experience in public health, having previously been based in the School of Primary Care and Public Health at Queen Mary, University of London where she led MSc modules on the social determinants of health. She held an MRC Population Health Scientist postdoctoral fellowship (2009–2012) with the aim of modelling diet and health inequalities using small-area estimation. Her substantive areas of research include food access, food insecurity, diet-related health, environmental influences on health and collaborating with public sector and civil society partners to develop novel area-based indicators of social inequality. Dianna (with Claire) developed a model of food insecurity risk used nationally in local government and contributes to JSNAs on food insecurity across local authorities, guiding data collection and analysis. These data, alongside new area-based measures of economic risk from Covid are shared on a co-developed (with Sustain and local government colleagues) open access website. She is currently working on a project to assess any impact of food aid interventions on local population health in Wessex, England.

**Dr Claire Thompson** is a Senior Research Fellow in the Centre for Research in Public Health and Community Care (CRIPACC) at the University of Hertfordshire, having previously been based at the London School of Hygiene and Tropical Medicine and, before that, Queen Mary University of London. She is a qualitative researcher who has worked on a variety of topics including Olympic regeneration, food environments, and local alcohol licencing. Claire's focus is dietary health inequalities and, in particular, food poverty and food practices in low-income neighbourhoods. She, along with Dianna, has worked with a range of local authorities on food poverty action plans and related strategies. She is currently the senior researcher for the Prevention and Early Detection in Health and Social Care research theme of the NIHR Applied Research Collaboration for the East of England. After completing a study on the impacts of COVID-19 on food and eating, she is currently working on a project team looking at the dietary health challenges for families with No Recourse to Public Funds.

# Acknowledgements

CT is funded by the National Institute for Health Research (NIHR) Applied Research Collaboration East of England.

Some work reported in this book was funded by NIHR ARC Wessex and consultancy projects for DS.

The views expressed are those of the author(s) and not necessarily those of the NIHR or the Department of Health and Social Care.

# 1 The complexities and challenges of researching hunger in wealthier countries

## Hunger in wealthy countries

The level of income inequality in the US and UK is well documented and is linked to poorer health outcomes in both countries (1). This link is partly explained by the way low incomes constrain and decrease choices around health-promoting behaviours such as maintaining a good quality diet. Inequality poses structural and material barriers to health and, therefore, can aptly be described as a social determinant of health (2). Low income contributes substantially to household food security in wealthier countries, through a variety of direct and indirect mechanisms.

The last few decades have chronicled a rise in challenges around food in wealthier countries (by which we mean high-income countries, as described by the World Bank (3)). Famine and hunger in poorer countries have long been the topic of global debates and appeals. People experiencing hunger in wealthier countries, like the US and the UK, have done so as a result of inequality, not famine resulting from food scarcity. Wealthier countries waste more than enough food to feed those who cannot afford to feed themselves. The UK alone throws away nearly 10 million tonnes of food every year (4), which raises controversies and questions. Discourse around the growing food aid sector, including food banks, soup kitchens, and food pantries, is testament to this. Poverty in wealthier countries, and by extension food poverty, is an inherently political issue (5).

It is widely agreed that food insecurity is difficult to measure, where it is measured at all, and that it is typically underestimated and under-reported. The most recent data from the UK, which asked respondents to comment on the last 30 days, suggests that 8% of UK households were food insecure in 2020 (6). The Food Foundation, a leading charity, found even higher rates – up to 9.7% – when they asked people about the six months from Summer 2020 to January 2021 (7). In the US, where such data are collected annually by the US Department of Agriculture, the prevalence is higher still, at

DOI: 10.4324/9781003184560-1

10.5% for 2020 (made up of 6.6% of households having *low food security* and 3.9% reporting *very low food security*) (8).

These data are based on surveys, meaning that only a sample of the wider population are asked. Of that sample, not everyone will respond and, of those that do, not all will interpret the questions in the way the researchers intended. Therefore, while acting as a useful barometer, these data are unlikely to convey the true number of people who are struggling to feed themselves and their families well, rather than scraping together lower quality diets.

## Food waste and surplus

As we will see, the typical support given to people who are food insecure are food parcels provided by the food aid sector, normally from food banks or similar services. The source of this food is often 'surplus' donations by manufacturers or supermarkets where items are mislabelled or in excess of what can be sold. Other sources include donations from the public to food banks, either of ambient goods or cash that can be used to purchase food to distribute. These mechanisms of sourcing and redistributing surplus food are usually framed as a way of reducing food waste because the 'waste' is given to people who cannot afford to buy enough food for themselves and their families. Unsurprisingly, this framing has attracted much criticism, not least because it is a poor substitute for government action on inequality to raise living standards for the poorest households and guarantee a right to food (9).

Supermarkets generate excessive and rising amounts of food waste and donating some of it to redistribution charities is both a way of trying to reduce that waste and a means of demonstrating corporate social responsibility (10). In the UK, the preeminent food waste charity is FareShare and in the US there are similar organisations like City Harvest (in New York). These charities do important work, redistributing enough food for millions of meals each year, as do the frontline charities and community groups working with those experiencing hunger to provide immediate relief. However, it remains a controversial approach. There is no evidence that redistributing surplus or wasted food addresses hunger and it may even serve to normalise and depoliticise hunger – inadvertently positioning it as a problem related to the distribution of food (9), rather than the unequal distribution of wealth and resources. Added to which, food waste is an important issue in its own right (Ibid).

The (re)distribution of surplus food can be understood in terms of pragmatic responses to symptoms of structural inequalities. Food waste and food aid charities readily state that their work is not an adequate or even desirable response to food insecurity. However, it is often the only response on offer. Food aid provides structures and mechanisms through which multiple actors and sectors can collaborate to address food insecurity.

## Food as poverty relief

Rising levels of hunger and the growth of the food aid sector, especially food banks, have been linked to cuts in public spending and welfare reform (11–13). As the state has retreated and support for the vulnerable and marginalised has diminished, food banks have expanded to try and fill the gap. Primarily, this has been by providing food as a form of poverty relief.

However, it has not been enough to stem the tide. Inequality and poverty continue to rise in wealthier countries and while food banks have an important role in providing immediate relief for severe (food) deprivation, they have little capacity to improve overall food insecurity outcomes due to the limited availability and provision of nutritious foods (14). Further, critics have positioned the food bank movement as an exemplar of the nexus of state retreat, precarity, and volunteerism, and one that forms a de facto non-state welfare safety net (15). While food banks, individually, can provide safety, support, and refuge for those experiencing extreme hardship (16), as a sector they can be viewed as inadvertently perpetuating a neo-liberal anti-welfare agenda based on conditionality and mistrust of cash-based welfare (15).

Twenty years ago, when food banks had only just started to appear in the UK, Graham Riches cautioned against an uncritical drift towards their institutionalisation, which would allow the government to rely on them as providers of residual 'last resort' support for those failed by the welfare state (17). And yet, this is exactly what has happened.

## Our approach: what this book does

As outlined above, hunger and inequality in wealthier countries, like the UK, is inherently political. The de facto response, food banks, is controversial and problematic. Added to which, food insecurity and food poverty are contested and problematic terms. They are symptomatic of severe economic and social inequalities and represent only part of the varied aspects of contemporary experiences of poverty and marginalisation. These issues are the subject of important debates and significant research undertakings across a range of disciplines, many of which are referenced in this book. Our aim, however, is not to further these debates. As they continue to unfold and develop in the academic, public, and policy spheres, the day-to-day necessity of mapping, understanding, and responding to food insecurity at the local level remains. That is not to say that local-level research is not informed by these developments, and vice versa. Nevertheless, professionals, volunteers, community groups, and the academics who collaborate with them have to bridge the gap between the national and the local and work with and around the moral contradictions and challenges that community-based research on food insecurity entails. Our aim is to contribute to those efforts by focusing on the concepts, debates, and methods that inform them. Our focus is the UK, but we make frequent reference and comparison to North America to contextualise.

### *In summary*

**Chapter 2:** explains the concept of **food deserts** and charts the development of food deserts research in the UK and North America. It tackles the topics of access and affordability and sets out how they can be measured.

**Chapter 3:** reviews the emergence and development of **food poverty** (and food insecurity) as a topic of research in the UK. While policy attention around the issue in the US can be traced back to the 1930s, it is only in the last decade that it has been the subject of widespread debate in the UK.

**Chapter 4:** presents a **conceptual framework** to support applied research. We explore key drivers of food insecurity through the lens of the social determinants of health and go on to examine the local resources and interventions that enable coordinated and potentially effective efforts to mitigate it.

**Chapter 5:** outlines differing **research methodologies** in practice, through exemplar studies of food access and food insecurity. We argue for research that brings together quantitative and qualitative methods and set out a process that can be followed to study the drivers and scale of food insecurity at the local level.

**Chapter 6:** concludes with a call to extend the well-rehearsed analyses of areas as food deserts and individuals as experiencing food insecurity. We then reflect on emerging debates and directions for research and policy.

### Key terms

As we outline and discuss the available research in the wider topic of food insecurity, it is helpful to start by defining key terms we use throughout this book.

- **Conceptual frameworks:** these are used to illustrate relationships between outcomes and factors which may influence these outcomes (18). Here we develop one to support research, but they are also useful for intervention planning to consider which population groups to target with an activity.

- **Household food insecurity:** this is differentiated from national or global food security which is often influenced by trade agreements and climate, or natural disasters. Here we follow the example of Dowler to define household food insecurity as the inability to access a diet of sufficient nutritional quality through socially acceptable means (19).
- **Food poverty:** the term is often used interchangeably with food insecurity. There are a range of definitions offered by charities and academics. It is neatly summed up by Tim Lang as: "worse diet, worse access, worse health, higher percentage of income on food and less choice from a restricted range of foods" (20).
- **Food deserts:** are areas where access to healthy and affordable food is limited, typically urban areas with a lower income population (21). Key authors include Daniel Block and Kimberly Morland in the US, Steve Cummins and Elizabeth Dowler in the UK. Early research originated in geography departments but also included public health researchers as the work extended to explore possible implications for population health.
- **Food stamps/vouchers:** in the US, a type of welfare provided to households where the funds may be used to purchase food only and is administered through the Supplemental Nutrition Assistance Program (SNAP) (22). In the UK, food vouchers may be provided by local government to households to purchase food items in some stores, the scheme was supported by Edenred to help families who normally access free school meals during the 2020 pandemic.
- **Impact evaluation:** is an assessment of how an intervention affects (typically health and economic) outcomes and whether these effects were intended or unintended. It measures the 'success' of interventions.
- **'Mapping':** in many instances, we are describing the geographic mapping of resources. However, there are situations where asset mapping is done with area residents in participatory processes to collectively identify the opportunities available to them – in which case this would be a list of useful services, a brief description, and their locations.
- **Obesogenic environments:** these are environments (including built, physical, and social environments) which promote excess body weight in the population. Traditionally the focus has been on residential environments, however, there is more work on other areas like the workplace or school. Key authors include Boyd Swinburn and colleagues, in Australia, who developed the concept.
- **Health inequalities:** refer to differences in health outcomes between or within populations and are often driven by social inequalities. In the US these are sometimes called health disparities (and now in England with the Office for Health Disparities and Improvement).

- **Poverty premiums:** are the excess costs incurred of being poorer and unable to access better options for credit, insurance, energy costs. Also, part of locational disadvantage and having to shop at more expensive places for food. See Beck's 2020 chapter for a full discussion (23).
- **Process evaluation:** is an assessment to determine whether the activities within an intervention (like a scheme, policy, or programme) were implemented as intended. It also investigates any barriers encountered, potential changes needed, and why the desired outcomes were or were not achieved (24).
- **Right to food:** the right to food is a campaign supported by civil society and academics to highlight the fact that, while the UK Government has ratified treaties which support this human right, it has yet to enshrine them in law across the four UK nations. Just Fair is a leading charity and campaigner on the issue (25).
- **Social Determinants of Health:** these are the social and economic influences on individual or population health that are social rather than biological. They are factors like housing, income, and education that influence health over the life course. The Social Determinants of Health (SDH) are described well by Sir Michael Marmot in the 2008 report for the World Health Organization (WHO) where they are noted as being driven by inequalities in money, power, and resources (26).

## References

1. Pickett K, Wilkinson R. *The spirit level*. Penguin Books; 2010.
2. Macintyre S. The Black Report and beyond: what are the issues? *Social Science & Medicine*. 1997;44(6):723–45.
3. Hamadeh N, Van Rompaey C, Metreau E. *New World Bank Country classifications by income level: 2021–2022*. World Bank; 2021. Available from: https://blogs.worldbank.org/opendata/new-world-bank-country-classifications-income-level-2021-2022.
4. Waste and Resources Action Programme (WRAP). *Food surplus and waste in the UK: key facts*. WRAP; 2020.
5. Lister R. *Poverty*. Polity; 2004.
6. Department for Environment Food and Rural Affairs. *United Kingdom food security report 2021*. Department for Environment Food and Rural Affairs; 2021.
7. The Food Foundation. *The impact of Covid-19 on household food security*. 2021.
8. U.S. Department of Agriculture Economic Research Service. *Food security in the US: key statistics & graphics*. Available from: https://www.ers.usda.gov/topics/food-nutrition-assistance/food-security-in-the-u-s/key-statistics-graphics/.

9.   Caraher M, Furey S. Is it appropriate to use surplus food to feed people in hunger? Short-term Band-Aid to more deep-rooted problems of poverty. *Food Research Collaboration.* 2017.

10.   Swaffield J, Evans D, Welch D. Profit, reputation and 'doing the right thing': Convention theory and the problem of food waste in the UK retail sector. *Geoforum.* 2018;89:43–51.

11.   Lambie-Mumford H, Green MA. Austerity, welfare reform and the rising use of food banks by children in England and Wales. *Area.* 2017;49(3):273–9.

12.   Tarasuk V, Dachner N, Loopstra R. Food banks, welfare, and food insecurity in Canada. *British Food Journal.* 2014;116(9):1405–17.

13.   Lambie-Mumford H, Loopstra R. Food banks and the UK welfare state. In: Lambie-Mumford H, Silvasti T, editors. *The rise of food charity in Europe.* Policy Press; 2020.

14.   Bazerghi C, McKay FH, Dunn M. The role of food banks in addressing food insecurity: a systematic review. *Journal of Community Health.* 2016;41(4):732–40.

15.   Briggs S, Foord M. Food banks and the transformation of British social welfare. *Czech & Slovak Social Work/Sociální Práce/Sociálna Práca.* 2017;17(4):72–86.

16.   Cloke P, May J, Williams A. The geographies of food banks in the meantime. *Progress in Human Geography.* 2016;41(6):703–26.

17.   Riches G. Food banks and food security: welfare reform, human rights and social policy. Lessons from Canada? *Social Policy and Administration.* 2002;36(6):648–63.

18.   Paradies Y, Stevens M. Conceptual diagrams in public health research. *Journal of Epidemiology and Community Health.* 2005;59(12):1012–3.

19.   Dowler EA, Kneafsey M, Lambie H, Inman A, Collier R. Thinking about 'food security': engaging with UK consumers. *Critical Public Health.* 2011;21(4):403–16.

20.   Sustain. What is food poverty? 2022 Available from: https://www.sustainweb.org/foodpoverty/whatisfoodpoverty/.

21.   Beaumont J, Lang T, Leather S, Mucklow C. *Report from the policy sub-group to the nutrition task force low income project team of the department of health.* Institute of Grocery Distribution; 1995.

22.   USDA Food and Nutrition Service. *Supplemental nutrition assitance program (SNAP).* 2021 Available from: https://www.fns.usda.gov/snap/supplemental-nutrition-assistance-program.

23.   Beck D. Poverty premiums: cost of being poor. In: Leal Filho W, Azul AM, Brandli L, Lange Salvia A, Özuyar PG, Wall T, editors. *No poverty.* Springer International Publishing; 2020. p. 1–13.

24.   Linnan L, Steckler A. *Process evaluation for public health interventions and research: an overview.* Wiley; 2002.

25.   Fair J. 2021. Available from: https://justfair.org.uk/campaigns-2/right-to-food/.

26.   World Health Organization. *Closing the gap in a generation: health equity through action on the social determinants of health - Final report of the commission on social determinants of health.* World Health Organization; 2008

# 2 Food deserts

## Access, affordability, and availability of retail food

*Dianna Smith*

## Introduction

One day in 2002 I was in Oregon (USA) listening to National Public Radio (NPR) and a story was shared about new vouchers for people accessing food stamps as part of the Women, Infants, and Children (WIC) scheme (1), a federal grant programme to provide supplemental foods for low-income pregnant, breastfeeding, postpartum women, and children up to age five on low incomes. The usual WIC offering was a redeemable coupon to be used in standard retail stores for milk, cheese, peanut butter and a range of other items. This newer option was to extend use of WIC vouchers to farmers markets and, thereby, obtain fresh produce. At the time, I was a student and this new provision led me to rethink my plans for my upcoming Masters thesis. I had originally intended to study the nutrient content of food grown organically or conventional agriculture. After hearing this story, I knew I wanted to learn more about food insecurity and what could be done to support people to have a healthy diet. I wanted to talk to people using the scheme and find out about their experiences and if the newer form of WIC supported a healthier diet. Plan A did not work out, but it led me to plan B: collecting data on the cost of food and locations of food stores in the local area, to see if there was an equal distribution of affordable and healthy food (2).

I am immensely grateful that I lacked the time and experience to follow through with the required ethics application that would have allowed me to go and interview women using the WIC project, because plan B started me on the path to researching food access and working in collaboration with local groups. In this case it was the Lane County Food Coalition in Oregon. Twenty years on, this approach to local data collection and collaboration is still a valuable research tool. But where did this concern for equitable access to healthy food begin, at least for academic research?

In this chapter, I will review the literature on food deserts and assess the evidence for them with a specific focus on the UK and the US. The core

DOI: 10.4324/9781003184560-2

aspects of food deserts (and by extension the less emotive term of food access) are applicable to other geographical research in access to services. I connect these themes of access and review the methodological innovation that is ongoing to measure access to both healthy and unhealthy food, as the research focus has evolved since the 1990s. Food deserts will be discussed in terms of the retail food environment (usually food shops). However, we acknowledge that other sources of food have become important in recent years, particularly food aid outlets such as food banks. The conceptual framing of food deserts used here is rooted in the social determinants of health, in particular the structural factors (distance to store and the cost of food, choice of food) and to a lesser extent, the behavioural influences on health. We should consider the work of Krieger (3) to explore the social ecological model, acknowledging the range of factors and scales of influences on food availability (and by extension, possibly health).

## What is a food desert?

The concept of food deserts has its origins the 1990s in the UK, where they were defined as "poor urban areas where residents cannot buy healthy and affordable food" (4). A paper by Mooney, which described the higher cost of food in poorer areas of London, captured the attention of policymakers from the mid-1990s (5) and the notion of food deserts subsequently influenced the Social Exclusion Unit in the UK (6). Thirty years later, there is still a tremendous level of discussion about the idea of poor access to food in certain areas of our towns and cities.

Food desert is a compelling and emotive phrase. It describes areas, usually in cities, where there was poor access, measured geographically, to healthy and affordable food. Notably, 'affordable' did not necessarily have a fixed financial boundary, as the cost of living and wages varied across different areas of the UK. Access was the first component of identifying possible food deserts, with two other factors of affordability and availability of healthy food the other considerations. Cost and availability will be discussed below, we will begin by exploring the measure of *access* and how this has changed over time.

## Access

Access was typically described as 500m walking distance to a food store as this was the distance that could be easily walked in 6–7 minutes (cited in Furey, Strugnell, & McIleveen 2001). These distances were often measured using Geographic Information Systems (GIS) where a 'buffer' of 500m would be placed around a store, and areas that were outside of this boundary and in relatively low-income neighbourhoods (definitions varied; (7, 8)) were considered to have 'poor access' and, therefore, be a potential food desert.

To have such a clear definition of distance or, at the very least, to define the access dimension of food deserts was an attractive prospect. We see similar distance-based measures in policy, such as the focus on access to greenspace to support population (physical and mental) health; here the distance of interest is 300m to an area of at least 2 hectares, referred to as the Accessible Natural Greenspace Standard (ANGSt) (9). This positivist approach is not without critics as there is a lack of nuance in the sharp boundary proposed (10, 11) and a one size fits all approach. Very quickly researchers worked to at least acknowledge the limitations of this distance measure (10), even if the solutions were not easily present. For example, there should be greater consideration of how someone accesses a store. The walking distance is sensible on one hand, but for people with mobility issues or small children, this may not be suitable. How easy is it to carry home a substantial amount of groceries over any distance? Where does this leave the larger, out of town supermarkets that are not easily accessible to pedestrians? These questions led to ideas such as including access to public transport (which would incur some cost) or thinking about household access to cars to facilitate travelling further distances.

Take a moment to reflect on how you access food in shops and the influences of your store choice – what format of store, mode of travel, impact of opening hours, caring responsibilities – to see where challenges emerge with this early model of food deserts.

A systematic review of measuring the *food environment* from 2007 provides an excellent overview of the research to that time on several aspects of the food environment in local areas, from presence of stores to basket comparisons and menu analyses (12). A complementary systematic review of *food deserts* was published in 2007 by Beaulac and colleagues (13) and another in 2010 with a focus on the US (14). Together these papers offer a substantial introduction to the idea of food deserts and food access, and are recommended to readers who want to explore the literature in more depth.

Simply looking at distance to a store does not reflect the actual access to retail food that people experience. Presence or absence of a store within a set distance or an administrative boundary is one quick approach to assessing physical access. In the next section we will look at the considerations needed to capture a wider measure of realistic access.

## Measuring geographic access

As stated above, typical distance measures for food access were problematic as they did not always take into account aspects such as the spaces someone could actually walk. Later researchers modified the approach, as technology advanced and enabled access to better data, by measuring the distances along road networks (15, 16) to show where someone may realistically travel on foot. In the US, academics measured access in cities using administrative units like census tracts as a proxy measure of a neighbourhood. These same areas form the basis of a national atlas of food access provided by the United States Department of Agriculture *Food Access Research Atlas* (17). In the UK, access was measured using a range of distances, as will be discussed below (7).

Geographic access is central to the idea of a food desert; economic access is secondary and collected under 'affordability'. This focus on spatial access is the main critique of work by Widener (11) where the use of longstanding approaches to assessing distance to healthy food sources was scrutinised. The question of how to accurately represent spatial access is an established point of consideration. For example, a methodological comparison of six approaches to measuring geographic access was completed in 2016 and concluded that the choice of measure had a clear impact on the results. The authors recommend that future research should test for correlations between access and health outcomes. Similar conclusions were drawn from a methodological comparison in the UK (18) and a methodological review in 2010 (19). However, as we will see later, this approach is not without its challenges (20).

In geographic terms, it is important to think about the starting point in measuring distance to food stores. This could be the population-weighted centroid of an administrative unit, or an average of distances from addresses within an area to a store. Researchers may opt to measure access to the nearest store of a minimum size, to reflect the likelihood of lower prices, availability of fresh produce and range of choice. When such analyses are undertaken at a national or state level, typically there is a trade-off with less detail used to allow for available computational power. For example, if food access were measured for a state in the US, the starting point (origin) is likely to be the geographic or population-weighted centroid of a census tract with the destination the nearest store of a minimum size, such as a supermarket (21). However, if the analysis undertaken is for one city within a state, then the origin can be more spatially precise, such as centroids of smaller administrative units or even address points (22). A thorough overview of the various means to measure access using GIS is provided in Burgoine et al. (18).

A consideration in any study is the quality of data for the retail food store locations. Often the main source is environment registers of premises selling food (21, 23), supplemented by ground-truthing (where locations are visited in person to assess the accuracy of records, such as for the store type or name and whether it is still open) exercises to check the reliability of datasets (24). In the UK, national datasets such as the Points of Interest were found to be of comparable quality in one small study (25). The idea that a larger store also offers unhealthy food and low prices is often overlooked in food desert research, but it is noted in food environment studies where retail food options are characterised as 'good' and 'bad' (26).

National-level analysis for the US, provided by the Economic Research Service through the Food Access (formerly Food Desert) Research Atlas, measures access to the nearest supermarket up to 10 and 20 miles in rural areas (17). This resource uses census tracts to approximate neighbourhoods and characterises those which are low income (based on one of three criteria, such as a poverty rate of 20% or higher) and also low access (a significant number of residents are more than a set distance to the nearest large grocery outlet). Full details are outlined in the documentation, but data from this atlas are increasingly used in the US for food access studies (17).

Further evolution of the access measure can be found in the use of spatial interaction models, led by the University of Leeds in the UK (27). These models of access originate in economics and in concepts applied by Christaller and Von Thunen about proximity and demand for services. One spatial interaction model applied to food desert modelling in the UK took account of consumer preference rather than simply measuring distance to the nearest store. It included the ability to stratify consumers into broad social groups and consider their expected shopping preferences, based on published company reports, to more accurately model food access and food deserts in UK cities including Cardiff and Leeds (27). With these models, the assumption remained that people started and ended their journeys to purchase groceries at home, an approach which persists. Later in this chapter we will outline the further developments of improved measures of geography away from residential areas and discrete zones, which started in part with spatial interaction models.

## Affordability

In the UK, significant focus is currently on low-income populations who experience food insecurity as a result of financial constraints. By comparison, thinking about the problem in terms of low spatial access has dropped off the radar somewhat. This is likely because the issue of food insecurity/poverty (see Chapter 3) has gained public and policy attention to become the dominant lens through which the inability to afford food is studied.

The cost of food, in particular food that makes up a healthy diet, is a core concern in the identification of an area as a food desert. The 1990 paper by Mooney used the comparison of a shopping basket of goods to demonstrate the difference in cost for similar food in socially contrasting area. Donkin and colleagues continued this theme and added consideration of foods appropriate for different ethnic groups (7). What was absent in the UK was a standardised 'shopping basket' which enabled direct comparison of costs in a range of stores, store formats (corner shop, supermarkets) and locations – more or less socially deprived.

Similar work was conducted in the US (28), where there was a standardised basket of food, the US Department of Agriculture (USDA) Thrifty Food Plan, that could be used for direct comparison of costs between different stores. The Thrifty Food Plan is used to calculate the monetary value of US Supplemental Nutrition Assistance Program (SNAP) benefits which are available to families on a low income for the purchase of food and household goods (see (29)).

Overall, affordability remains a core consideration in exploring the factors which influence diet quality (and by extension, health). This type of analysis continues in many areas (30), often led by people working in public health or nutrition to provide a baseline measure of the food costs and opportunities available in local areas. In the UK there has been a re-emergence of food basket comparisons within smaller areas or a city, often following the interest of local government teams who seek to understand the possible influences on household food insecurity, which will be discussed in the following chapter.

Comparative food baskets have been developed and adapted as required; in the case of Block and Kouba, the USDA Thrifty Food Plan was modified to include items relevant to the local community (here, sweet potatoes, greens and infant formula) while keeping the standard list intact to allow for comparison elsewhere (30). This localised approach works effectively in smaller areas such as a city or rural district to enable community-specific comparisons. Baskets may include non-food items to reflect the need for regular purchases of toiletries such as nappies/diapers, toilet roll or toothpaste.

The size of a store impacts on the cost of food available, with evidence to show that prices are lower in larger stores, and the abundance of smaller format shops like convenience stores contributes to affordable options in neighbourhoods. This is evident in both the US (28) and the UK (31).

## Beyond food cost in place: higher-level inequalities in cost

Researchers in the US and then the UK have developed and applied various approaches to demonstrate the higher cost of healthier foods. Drewnowski and colleagues completed a cost comparison on key food items, not to identify food deserts but to assess the relative cost of healthy and less healthy food items (32). This was replicated in the UK (33) and the result was similar – to maintain a healthy diet (as defined by the respective national governments) – people need to pay more for food, and for people on lower incomes it requires an even larger proportion of their 'disposable' income. As we will see in Chapter 3, this difference in cost between healthy and less healthy foods contributes to the outcome in lower income households of food insecurity or food poverty; when one aspect of the household budget (food) is naturally more elastic, this is where savings can be most easily made. Further work is now needed to understand what people actually purchase, as is collected in national level surveys such as the Living Costs and Food Survey in the UK or smaller studies (22).

## Standardised measures

Measurement of food deserts was standardised, in some way, in both the US and the UK. In the US this took the form of tools made available by the USDA which are available online (17). The UK does not have a standard tool supported by the government, however, there were academic approaches outlined in 2017 by Wilkins and colleagues to create a uniform approach to measuring retail food environments (34). Their paper summarised the available methods and recommended a checklist for researchers to apply when reporting measures of the retail food environment.

Further developments in the UK include a newer E-food Desert Index (35). Due to scale, these national level measures often require a relatively simple method, similar to the USDA measure of food access. This national index includes consideration of distance and density of retail food outlets, transport and local population characteristics, access to online shopping using the 2018 Internet User Classification·in small areas (Lower Super Output Areas or Data Zones, each with a population of about 1,500). Collectively, this brings together a standard measure of retail food access for England, Wales and Scotland. Local level research can identify other pressures that may concern residents, such as the variety of foods and opening hours of the retail sources or availability of private and public transportation options.

## Improving access measures

Critical reviews suggest the need for innovation in food access/food desert research, especially when defining or measuring access. In 2013, Black and colleagues noted that the evidence for inequalities in food access in the US (compared to other wealthy countries) was most compelling (36), similar to findings by Cummins and Macintyre (37) in part due to the way data are collected (or are available). Overall, there is demand from numerous research teams for more nuanced measures of the food environment, access, or food deserts (38). Further work on relational geographies (10) and activity spaces (39) show the way forward for exploring relationships between area features and diet.

Here, the concern is that by confining people (in theory) to the areas immediate to their homes, we underestimate their access to stores; not all people shop at the nearest store (22). One way to account for these further travel distances is to address boundary or edge effects by extending the searchable area for retail outlets beyond the area of immediate interest. A wider study area such as this can be used to acknowledge movement outside of an area (21). Spatial interaction models also help to address this limitation.

Assessing the density of food options within administrative units such as census tracts or block groups, data zones or similar emerged as another option to measure access to retail food (19, 23). The benefit of this density measure is that it reflects the greater choices available to households locally. For households on a limited budget, the option to shop somewhere with lower costs can represent the difference between a more balanced and healthy diet and a financially constrained situation where cheaper and less nutritious alternatives are selected. The flawed assumption about what is accessible remains if neighbourhoods are approximated by census tracts or similar units, as people do travel outside of their home areas.

A substantial innovation in the area of food deserts is aligned to the issues of physical access, by exploring the interaction of an individual with an environment. This has been advanced by Kestens and colleagues with research assessing the activity spaces of people, to identify individual areas of influence with regards to food environments and health outcomes (39). Though this is often conceptualised to measure exposure to unhealthy (fast food) environments, then underlying principles are relevant to food deserts as well. For example, if a person travels in one direction predominantly from their home, the presence of a supermarket 500m in the opposite direction is immaterial to their food access options. This also reflects the concept of a subjective food environment. A substantial review of the literature where food environments are assessed using GPS was provided in 2016, once again suggesting that symmetrical measures around the home environment were an inappropriate starting point for assessing realistic measures of food access (40).

Since this area of research developed in the 1990s, many changes have taken place in society such as the widespread availability of the internet and the subsequent rise of online shopping, including for food. We may consider the impact online shopping has on food access overall, however, the population of concern when studying food deserts or retail food access are lower income groups. These households may not have the financial resources to meet the minimum spending requirement for a home delivery of groceries, and may have limited access to the internet to support the process of online shopping. There are also delivery charges that will be unaffordable for people on the lowest incomes.

The ongoing focus on residential food environments as a main influence on diet overlooks the problem of lack of availability or means to travel further to increase affordable food options. This focus misses a key concern for economically constrained populations, which is why both distance to stores and cost of foods are important. However, when we consider diet quality as a predictor for health outcomes, other environments are also important such as where people work (41) or study (26).

## Availability

In order to calculate availability, and in the absence of a standardised basket of goods such as the Thrifty Food Plan, analyses would typically note the number and varieties available of healthier food items, usually fresh produce (31, 42). Repeatedly the finding would be that smaller format shops, such as convenience stores and corner shops, had poorer availability (36). The assumption behind this difference was down to the available storage for such goods and perceived consumer demand. The usual reason for poorer availability of fresh produce in smaller format stores was that produce would become inedible before it was purchased, causing the shop owner to dispose of it and lose income.

Some researchers noted the perceived quality of fresh produce in a range of shops and concluded that the smaller shops in parts of Scotland had poorer availability and poorer quality compared to larger stores and supermarkets (15). As described above, smaller format stores are also usually more expensive and more likely to be located in lower income/more deprived areas; this leads to greater disadvantage for people who rely on smaller local shops for their food.

## Food deserts – do they matter for health?

Once there was an established measure or process to identify food deserts (access, affordability, and availability in some combination), the next consideration was around health and related factors on the pathway to health, such as diet. For the ease of measurement, diet is often assessed via the portions of fruit and vegetables consumed each day by local residents (23, 43). If there are disparities in access to affordable and healthy retail food, that is a concern in terms of social or environmental justice. But the question remains as to how to engage with policy makers and people with the power to make changes? Public health and health inequalities between population groups was an obvious focal point. This shift to not just measuring the food environment in some way but also to explore an association with health in the resident population was part of the work in the Atherosclerosis in Communities study led by Morland and colleagues (23, 42). In this approach, there is an assumed relationship from area of residence food environment to diet quality then to health. This presumed relationship contributed to the developing discussions around obesogenic (obesity-promoting) environments (44); in the US this discussion is sometimes explored alongside issues of racial segregation (23, 42).

One influential piece of research considered the impact of food deserts, measured objectively based on distance and also subjectively (access as perceived by residents), and then assessed whether there was any relationship between food deserts and diet outcomes. As is often the case diet was measured on the basis of fruit and vegetable consumption. Here the results showed that people who did not perceive there to be a supermarket within walking distance of their home (who in fact had one within 1km) ate significantly less fruit and vegetables than people who did consider themselves living within a walking distance (45). As previously discussed, there is the need to better understand where people shop for food and move beyond the assumption that many people complete their regular food shop near to where they live. Research in the US shows mixed results and, in some examples, it is known that people travel well away from their homes (when they have access to a car) to reach larger stores and lower prices (22).

Rather than investigating the potential of food deserts as a cause for poor health outcomes, some studies have looked at the impact of living in a food desert on maintaining health. More recent literature from the US brings food deserts in as a consideration for recovering from ill health and readmission to hospital. Patients living in food deserts had poorer health outcomes (46, 47). However, this line of research must consider the length of exposure to unhealthy food options and how long it takes to develop poor health outcomes. After all people do move home! In most studies we do not know how long someone has lived in a food desert, and we also do not know how long they spend in their home neighbourhood compared to work, school or social environments. Longitudinal research is needed to identify the length of time a person lives in a food desert with health outcomes that can develop over the same time period. For these reasons, outcomes with short time frames like hospital readmission are more relevant. In most cases, the outcomes will be influenced by more than just diet, as we see with conceptual models of obesity causation (48).

The food desert idea is modified in the context of obesogenic environments, specifically when retail food options are measured. An obesogenic environment is an environment of varying scales that encourages excess weight through influences on diet and physical activity (44). Put simply, it encourages people to consume unhealthy foods and engage in less physical activity. Inherently, the retail food environment is a key aspect of identifying an area as obesity-promoting in the population; again, the resident population is usually the focus. It should be noted that this emphasis is largely a result of data availability, and with greater access to personalised GPS data and trip/travel data, researchers are more able to model where people are exposed to both positive and less healthy food environments. One such piece of research identified that more exposure to fast food outlets was associated with higher BMI (41).

Food access should also be considered in association with racial inequality, and how this can exacerbate social inequalities. In the example of healthy food, prices are lower in supermarkets, so not having one nearby is a challenge for affordable food options (28). Research in the US concluded that lower income neighbourhoods have poorer availability of larger format stores (with lower prices on healthy foods and greater choice), and that there were also observable differences in access between categories of food outlet density of non-white populations in neighbourhoods (21, 42, 49). In addition, there were more fast food options in low income neighbourhoods and these differences were divided similarly along ethnic characteristics of neighbourhoods (50). This disadvantage in access may contribute to associated health inequalities over time if people remain in neighbourhoods with poorer access, higher costs or lower availability of choice. This type of structural barrier to healthy food may be added to individual barriers that are discussed in the following chapter and contributes to our conceptual framework.

## Summary

After 30 years, the idea of a food desert maintains such traction that the description of an area as 'desert' now extends to areas lacking affordable social care ('care deserts' (51)) and areas where unhealthy food (such as fast food) is abundant and healthy food lacking are 'food swamps' (52). The earliest work in this field captured a range of spatial access, cost and availability data, often for neighbourhoods or a city. Over time we have improved technology for mapping data such as store locations and areas of residence, and also questioned the focus on homes as the starting point for food deserts, with the nearest store the assumed destination. The availability of personalised activity patterns (22, 39) reinforced the need to consider access more subjectively (10). In both the US and UK there were reviews of the methods and, notably, some products were developed to offer national-level atlases of food deserts/measures of access (17, 35).

There have been calls to 'retire' the food desert metaphor, largely as it is overly simplistic (11). However, the core concepts associated with this notion of food deserts offer value to organisations seeking to explore local area influences on diet choices, which in turn is connected theoretically to an array of health outcomes (53). Aligned ideas are a 'postcode lottery' of access to services from health care (54); these are implicitly about environmental justice. At the heart of food deserts is the idea of locational disadvantage, that where one lives will influence their social or health outcomes, reflecting a component of the social determinants of health that lies outside of individual characteristics. This idea is neatly shown in the Dahlgren and Whitehead model of social determinants of health (55), where individual determinants lie at the centre of the model and local (access to services) then wider influences (healthcare structure, welfare policy) are in rings moving further from the person. Whether someone has capacity to easily move from the area they live within is often associated with their socioeconomic position, if they have a car or access to public transport.

The reason food deserts continue to be a research and policy consideration is due to the potential that food access has to influence people's diets and associated health. As discussed, we cannot conclude that living in a food desert *causes* poor health due to the multiple influences on diet related health outcomes like obesity and type 2 diabetes and the lack of longitudinal research to measure length of exposure to a food environment. However, with the ongoing studies exploring relationships between food environments more broadly (fast food) and health, the evidence for associations especially in the US is stronger. Even without a direct causal pathway between living in a food desert and poorer diet related health, there remains the problem of environmental (in)justice for people without adequate access to healthy and affordable food. The choice to eat healthily needs to be available to everyone regardless of income, age, race, gender.

# References

1. Special Supplemental Nutrition Program for Women, Infants, and Children (WIC): USDA. Available from: https://www.fns.usda.gov/wic.
2. Smith DM. *Food deserts in the Willamette? A study of food access in Lane County*. Oregon State University; 2003.
3. Krieger N. *Epidemiology and the people's health: theory and context*. Oxford University Press; 2011.
4. Beaumont J, Lang T, Leather S, Mucklow C. *Report from the policy sub-group to the nutrition task force low income project team of the department of health*. Institute of Grocery Distribution; 1995.

5.  Mooney C. Cost and availability of healthy food choices in a London health district. *Journal of Human Nutrition and Dietetics.* 1990;3(2):111–20.

6.  Social Exclusion Unit S. *Bringing Britain together: a national strategy for neighbourhood renewal.* The Stationary Office Dobson et al Policy and Governance for Integrated Urban Sustainability; 1998.

7.  Donkin AJM, Dowler EA, Stevenson SJ, Turner SA. Mapping access to food at a local level. *British Food Journal.* 1999;101(7):554–64.

8.  Shaw HJ. Food deserts: towards the development of a classification. *Geografiska Annaler: Series B, Human Geography.* 2006;88(2):231–47.

9.  Natural England. *Accessible natural green space standards in towns and cities: a review and toolkit for their implementation. English Nature. 2003.*

10. Cummins S, Curtis S, Diez-Roux AV, Macintyre S. Understanding and representing 'place' in health research: a relational approach. *Social Science & Medicine* (1982). 2007;65(9):1825–38.

11. Widener MJ. Spatial access to food: retiring the food desert metaphor. *Physiology & Behavior.* 2018;193:257–60.

12. McKinnon RA, Reedy J, Morrissette MA, Lytle LA, Yaroch AL. Measures of the food environment: a compilation of the literature, 1990–2007. *American Journal of Preventive Medicine.* 2009;36(4) Supplement:S124–S33.

13. Beaulac J, Kristjansson E, Cummins S. A systematic review of food deserts, 1966–2007. *Preventing Chronic Disease.* 2009;6(3):A105.

14. Walker RE, Keane CR, Burke JG. Disparities and access to healthy food in the United States: A review of food deserts literature. *Health Place.* 2010;16(5):876–84.

15. Cummins S, Smith DM, Taylor M, Dawson J, Marshall D, Sparks L, et al. Variations in fresh fruit and vegetable quality by store type, urban-rural setting and neighbourhood deprivation in Scotland. *Public Health Nutrition.* 2009;12(11):2044–50.

16. Smith DM, Cummins S, Taylor M, Dawson J, Marshall D, Sparks L, et al. Neighbourhood food environment and area deprivation: spatial accessibility to grocery stores selling fresh fruit and vegetables in urban and rural settings. *International Journal of Epidemiology.* 2010;39(1):277–84.

17. Agriculture USDo. *Food access research atlas.* 2021 Available from: https://www.ers.usda.gov/data-products/food-access-research-atlas/.

18. Burgoine T, Alvanides S, Lake A. Creating 'obesogenic realities'; do our methodological choices make a difference when measuring the food environment? *International Journal of Health Geographics.* 2013;12(1):33.

19. Charreire H, Casey R, Salze P, Simon C, Chaix B, Banos A, et al. Measuring the food environment using geographical information systems: a methodological review. *Public Health Nutrition.* 2010;13(11):1773–85.

20. Jaskiewicz L, Block D, Chavez N. Finding food deserts: a comparison of methods measuring spatial access to food stores. *Health Promotion Practice.* 2016;17(3):400–7.

21. Zenk SN, Schulz AJ, Israel BA, James SA, Bao S, Wilson ML. Neighborhood racial composition, neighborhood poverty, and the spatial accessibility of

supermarkets in metropolitan Detroit. *American Journal of Public Health.* 2005;95(4):660–7.

22. Dubowitz T, Zenk SN, Ghosh-Dastidar B, Cohen DA, Beckman R, Hunter G, et al. Healthy food access for urban food desert residents: examination of the food environment, food purchasing practices, diet and BMI. *Public Health Nutrition.* 2015;18(12):2220–30.

23. Morland K, Wing S, Roux AD. The contextual effect of the local food environment on residents' diets: the atherosclerosis risk in communities study. *American Journal of Public Health.* 2002;92(11):1761–8.

24. Lake A, Burgoine T, Stamp E, Grieve R. The foodscape: classification and field validation of secondary data sources across urban/rural and socio-economic classifications in England. *International Journal of Behavioral Nutrition and Physical Activity.* 2012;9(1):37.

25. Burgoine T, Harrison F. Comparing the accuracy of two secondary food environment data sources in the UK across socio-economic and urban/rural divides. *International Journal of Health Geographics.* 2013;12(1):2.

26. Smith D, Cummins S, Clark C, Stansfeld S. Does the local food environment around schools affect diet? Longitudinal associations in adolescents attending secondary schools in East London. *BMC Public Health.* 2013;13(1):70.

27. Clarke G, Eyre H, Guy C. Deriving indicators of access to food retail provision in British cities: studies of Cardiff, Leeds and Bradford. *Urban Studies.* 2002;39(11):2041–60.

28. Chung C, Myers SL. Do the poor pay more for food? An analysis of grocery store availability and food price disparities. *Journal of Consumer Affairs.* 1999;33(2):276–96.

29. U.S. Department of Agriculture. *Thrifty food plan. Food and Nutrition Service.* 2021.

30. Block D, Kouba J. A comparison of the availability and affordability of a market basket in two communities in the Chicago area. *Public Health Nutrition.* 2006;9(7):837–45.

31. Cummins S, Smith DM, Aitken Z, Dawson J, Marshall D, Sparks L, et al. Neighbourhood deprivation and the price and availability of fruit and vegetables in Scotland. *Journal of Human Nutrition and Dietetics.* 2010;23(5):494–501.

32. Monsivais P, Drewnowski A. The rising cost of low-energy-density foods. *Journal of the American Dietetic Association.* 2007;107(12):2071–6.

33. Jones NRV, Conklin AI, Suhrcke M, Monsivais P. The growing price gap between more and less healthy foods: analysis of a novel longitudinal UK dataset. *PLOS ONE.* 2014;9(10):e109343.

34. Wilkins EL, Morris MA, Radley D, Griffiths C. Using geographic information systems to measure retail food environments: discussion of methodological considerations and a proposed reporting checklist (Geo-FERN). *Health Place.* 2017;44:110–7.

35. Newing A. *E-food desert index.* 2021. Available from: https://data.cdrc.ac.uk /dataset/e-food-desert-index.

36. Black C, Moon G, Baird J. Dietary inequalities: what is the evidence for the effect of the neighbourhood food environment? *Health Place*. 2014;27:229–42.

37. Cummins S, Macintyre S. Food environments and obesity: neighbourhood or nation? *International Journal of Epidemiology*. 2006;35(1):100–4.

38. Shearer C, Rainham D, Blanchard C, Dummer T, Lyons R, Kirk S. Measuring food availability and accessibility among adolescents: Moving beyond the neighbourhood boundary. *Social Science & Medicine* (1982). 2015;133:322–30.

39. Kestens Y, Lebel A, Chaix B, Clary C, Daniel M, Pampalon R, et al. Association between Activity Space Exposure to Food Establishments and Individual Risk of Overweight. *PLOS ONE*. 2012;7(8):e41418.

40. Cetateanu A, Jones A. How can GPS technology help us better understand exposure to the food environment? A systematic review. *SSM: Population Health*. 2016;2:196–205.

41. Burgoine T, Forouhi NG, Griffin SJ, Wareham NJ, Monsivais P. Associations between exposure to takeaway food outlets, takeaway food consumption, and body weight in Cambridgeshire, UK: population based, cross sectional study. *BMJ: British Medical Journal*. 2014;348:g1464.

42. Morland K, Filomena S. Disparities in the availability of fruits and vegetables between racially segregated urban neighbourhoods. *Public Health Nutrition*. 2007;10(12):1481–9.

43. Wrigley N, Warm D, Margetts B. Deprivation, diet, and food-retail access: findings from the leeds 'food deserts' study. *Environment and Planning A*. 2003;35(1):151–88.

44. Egger G, Swinburn B. An "ecological" approach to the obesity pandemic. *BMJ: British Medical Journal*. 1997;315(7106):477–80.

45. Caspi CE, Kawachi I, Subramanian SV, Adamkiewicz G, Sorensen G. The relationship between diet and perceived and objective access to supermarkets among low-income housing residents. *Social Science & Medicine* (1982). 2012;75(7):1254–62.

46. Morris AA, McAllister P, Grant A, Geng S, Kelli HM, Kalogeropoulos A, et al. Relation of living in a "food desert" to recurrent hospitalizations in patients with heart failure. *American Journal of Cardiology*. 2019;123(2):291–6.

47. Smith EJT, Ramirez JL, Wu B, Zarkowsky DS, Gasper WJ, Finlayson E, et al. Living in a food desert is associated with 30-day readmission after revascularization for chronic limb-threatening ischemia. *Annals of Vascular Surgery*. 2021;70:36–42.

48. Jones A, Bentham G, Foster C, Hilsdon M, Panter J. *Foresight tackling obesities: future choices – obesogenic environments – evidence review*. Government Office for Science; 2007.

49. Rummo PE, Guilkey DK, Ng SW, Popkin BM, Evenson KR, Gordon-Larsen P. Beyond supermarkets: food outlet location selection in four U.S. cities over time. *American Journal of Preventive Medicine*. 2017;52(3):300–10.

50. Hilmers A, Hilmers DC, Dave J. Neighborhood disparities in access to healthy foods and their effects on environmental justice. *American Journal of Public Health*. 2012;102(9):1644–54.

51. Power A, Bell SL, Kyle RG, Andrews GJ. 'Hopeful adaptation'in health geographies: seeking health and wellbeing in times of adversity. *Social Science & Medicine*. 2019;231:1–5.

52. Rose D, Bodor N, Swalm C, Rice J, Farley T, Hutchinson P. Deserts in New Orleans? *Illustrations of Urban Food access and Implications for Policy*. University of Michigan National Poverty Center; 2009.

53. Cummins S, Findlay A, Higgins C, Petticrew M, Sparks L, Thomson H. Reducing inequalities in health and diet: findings from a study on the impact of a food retail development. *Environment and Planning A: Economy and Space*. 2008;40(2):402–22.

54. Russell J, Greenhalgh T, Lewis H, Mackenzie I, Maskrey N, Montgomery J, et al. Addressing the 'postcode lottery' in local resource allocation decisions: a framework for clinical commissioning groups. *Journal of the Royal Society of Medicine*. 2013;106(4):120–3.

55. Dahlgren G, Whitehead M. *Policies and strategies to promote social equity in health. Background document to WHO-Strategy paper for Europe*. Institute for Futures Studies; 1991.

# 3 The emergence of 'food poverty' as a research topic

## Claire Thompson

## Introduction

The first time I heard the terms 'food poverty' and 'food bank' was in 2010, whilst investigating food practices in low-income neighbourhoods as part of my PhD fieldwork. I was interviewing local residents in a town in the Midlands, UK. I spoke to a very interesting woman about her voluntary work in the community and she told me that she worked in a food bank. I had to ask her to explain what that was. I remember being shocked that anyone in the UK would be unable to afford enough food (even cheap and poor-quality food) and thinking that it must be very unusual. I had read about food stamps and food insecurity in the North American context, but that seemed a world away from the UK. It is difficult to put into words how wrong I was about that.

The relationship between hunger and poverty in the UK was already being written about in the 1990s (1, 2). By the end of that decade more than 3,000 tonnes of surplus and donated food were being redistributed in the UK by various agencies, including food banks, every year (3). In fact, the ongoing and international rise of food aid (mostly in the form of charitable food banking) has long been anticipated (4). But while household food poverty has been a recognised social and public health issue in North America since the 1990s (5), it has taken longer to become the subject of public debate in the UK. It was not until 2010 that hunger, poverty and the rapid growth of food banks attracted substantial public, media, and policy concern (6). As we will see, a combination of financial and political factors brought the issue to a head in the UK.

## The relationship between food, poverty, and hunger

Public, political, moral, and academic debates around poverty and hunger have a long history. Portions of the world's population have often suffered

DOI: 10.4324/9781003184560-3

sustained periods of hunger caused by war, plagues, or adverse weather. Contemporary causes of hunger are predominantly related to climate, conflict, and economic crises (7). The first time hunger in the US gained significant public and policy attention was during the Great Depression of the 1930s, which left a quarter of the workforce unemployed and the country's farmers producing more food than they could profitably sell (8). In the modern era, lack of food production is rarely the reason that people are hungry. The United States continues to produce more food than the population needs and hunger remains a significant problem (9). The 'temporary' food stamp programme introduced in 1939 has undergone transformations and name changes (10), but is still in existence today (as the Supplemental Nutrition Assistance Programme – SNAP – described in Chapter 2) and has proved to be anything but temporary.

The UK, by comparison, is not self-sufficient in food production. It is a food-trading nation, both importing and exporting food. Food and soft drinks are the largest manufacturing sector in the UK (11). The year 2008 saw a financial crisis and a sharp rise in global food prices, pushing an additional 40 million people around the world into hunger (12). Low-and middle-income countries were the most severely affected (13). In wealthier countries, the spike in food prices impacted low-income households the hardest. It disproportionately inflated the prices of milk, eggs, and bread: staples that poorer families tend to spend more on. The spike brought an end to the long-standing decline in relative price of food in the UK (11).

Some countries, including the UK, reacted to the financial crisis of 2008 by implementing austerity measures: strict economic policies to reduce government spending and lower public debt. The austerity policies introduced in 2010 by the UK's Conservative and Liberal-Democrat coalition government comprised of a systematic programme of public spending cuts and tax rises aimed at reducing the budget deficit and helping the country recover from the effects of the financial crisis (14). Large scale cuts were made to central and local government budgets, welfare services, and benefits (15). UK austerity policies have been consistently linked to rising food insecurity and food bank use (16). Welfare reform, in particular, has heightened the need for food banks via changes to entitlement and inadequate administration processes that are punitive (17) and inefficient, leaving people without any benefits income for months on end (17). A decade of austerity policies has cut spending on welfare benefits by nearly a quarter, with working-age benefit levels stagnating or frozen and those living with disabilities disproportionately impacted (18).

The most direct impact of austerity has been on wages. Over the last ten years, real wage growth has slowed by an average of a half (19). This means that although wages have increased, this increase has not exceeded the growth in the cost of living. Therefore, earnings have effectively (in 'real terms') fallen (20). In-work poverty is a growing trend in the UK because earnings growth has been so low for so long that paid work cannot reliably lift households above the poverty line as it once did. In fact, household earnings growth for the lowest-paid is consistently below the average. Those on lower wages are now also much more likely to work part-time, further lowering their overall income (21). The pandemic looks to be compounding these challenges with a legacy of decreasing job insecurity and infringements of labour market rights (22). The resulting and sometimes chronic hardship has left evermore people unable to consistently meet their most basic nutritional needs

Poverty rates, including food poverty, have increased rapidly (15). These developments have led to growing public concern, mainstream media coverage, and increased policy attention (6). A media analysis of UK print media coverage of food banks found that, before 2008, there were no UK-focused articles about them. Overall, there were very few until 2012 when the numbers increased dramatically. These findings suggest that, around this time, the media moved from reporting UK food banks as something unusual and temporary towards their proliferation becoming the subject of ongoing concern and controversy (23)

## Food insecurity or food poverty?

*Food security* means having consistent physical, social, and economic access to sufficient, safe, and nutritious food that meets food preferences and dietary needs for an active and healthy life (24). Although originally used to characterise the nutritional status of nations, it is now widely used to refer to broader problems related to household food status.

*Household food insecurity* is limited or uncertain availability of nutritionally adequate and safe foods, or limited or uncertain ability to acquire acceptable foods in socially acceptable ways (25). Increased research focus on identifying and understanding the phenomenon in developed countries such as Canada, Australia, the United States, and the UK, has demonstrated that it is not exclusive to poorer countries and developing nations (26). Dowler defines *food poverty* as the opposite of food security, as the inability to acquire or consume adequate quality and quantities of food in socially acceptable ways, or experiencing uncertainty about being able to do so (27).

The terms food poverty and food insecurity are often used interchangeably (28, 29). This has certainly been my practice, depending on the audience, publication, or event I am preparing for. In applied policy and intervention settings, as we will see in Chapter 5, using the term 'food poverty' can be viewed as having political overtones, and 'food insecurity' is sometimes thought to be too opaque for non-specialist audiences.

However, overtones aside, food insecurity and food poverty are not technically the same thing. O'Connor et al.'s (2015) review of the terminology identifies four pillars of food insecurity: access, availability; utilisation, and stability. The distinction for food poverty can be identified when economic access (poverty) is the main component. Further, the authors posit that while food insecurity can exist without food poverty, food poverty cannot exist without food insecurity (30). Meaning that food poverty can be thought of as a type of food insecurity. For the remainder of this chapter the term food poverty is favoured, with its emphasis on economic access. In the UK, the most common recorded reason for visiting a food bank remains economic hardship caused by problems with welfare benefits (31, 32).

## Food poverty and health

Food poverty has varying degrees of severity ranging from worry about whether there will be enough food through to compromising quality and quantity, and then going without food and experiencing hunger (Taylor & Loopstra, 2016). In wealthier nations, where nutrient-poor processed foods are cheap and readily available (33), hunger rarely leads to starvation. Rather, it leads to malnutrition and, paradoxically, obesity. In order to maintain adequate energy intake, people who must limit food costs will select lower-quality diets, consisting of energy-dense, inexpensive foods. Such diets are associated with a range of conditions including hypertension, iron deficiency, impaired liver function, and poor oral health (33–36).

The relationship between food poverty and health is dynamic. Food poverty is a social determinant of health (37). Meaning that it influences health outcomes. Experiencing food poverty can worsen existing health problems and even cause new ones. This can amplify vulnerabilities and create a 'feedback loop': those with poor health are at increased risk of food poverty; the experience of food poverty worsens their health and increases morbidity; which in turn can further increase risk and/or the severity of food poverty (38, 39).

A pertinent example of this can be seen in the plight of those with severe mental illness (including Schizophrenia and Bipolar Disorder), who tend to have a shorter life expectancy compared to the general population and are at greater risk of obesity and food poverty. Living with constant worries about not getting enough food or facing chronic hunger leaves people unable to support their mental health and wellbeing (40), and so a deterioration of existing conditions and difficulty managing them can be expected (41).

For the last decade, food poverty has been widely described and acknowledged as a public health crisis in the UK (42–44) and the COVID-19 pandemic has only worsened the situation (45). Tackling public health problems, like food poverty, requires a detailed understanding of the nature and extent of those problems. At a national level, this means collecting data (surveillance) to find out and monitor aspects of the problem such as incidence, prevalence, and severity. In the US, national food security data have been collected every year since 1995 (46). In Canada, national surveys started asking questions about hunger in 1994. Since 2004, regular population monitoring on food poverty has occurred through the Canadian Community Health Survey (47). By comparison, the UK government has been much slower to implement a measure (48), despite wide-spread calls to do so for some years (43, 49, 50). Since April 2019, the Family Resource Survey has included questions on household food poverty (51). This is around ten years after the financial crisis, spike in global food prices, and implementation of austerity measures that led to a sharp rise in levels and awareness of food poverty.

## Food poverty and food banks

In the decade it took for the UK Government to institute a national measure of food poverty, a varied body of research including public health, social policy and geography, has sought to understand the nature, scale, extent, and severity of the phenomenon. Perhaps the most prominent example of this is research on food banks. A food bank is a non-profit charitable organisation that distributes donated and surplus food to those unable to access a sufficient quantity and quality of food, normally for reasons related to economic hardship. The US and Canada have a long history of charitable food provision and research examining it (52). Compared to North America, food banks are a relatively recent development in the UK (23). According to Sustain, an alliance of organisations working to improve the food system and tackle food poverty, there was only one reported food bank in the UK in the year 2000 (3).

In the UK, access to food banks is mediated via referral from front-line service providers such as GPs, Job Centre staff, and Family Support Workers (53). Once a referral is obtained, the individual can then obtain a food parcel, providing enough food for a few days or even a week. Identifying and counting food banks is challenging. The term 'food bank' is widely used and understood, but there is significant variability in the types of services, processes, and food stuffs provided by the organisations that are identified as such (54). Some food banks are hubs that distribute food to smaller food banks that might not be listed. Others may have a different primary function – such as a community centre – but operate a food bank service as a secondary, temporary, or occasional function. The Independent Food Aid Network (IFAN) estimate that there are now at least 1,172 independent food banks and 1,393 Trussell Trust food banks operating across the UK (55).

Food banks have come to dominate and define food poverty debates and discourses in the UK (54). There is a substantial body of qualitative research exploring experiences and dynamics within food banks and around the practices of food banking. Food banks can be spaces of care and support (56) and function as social spaces (15) in which volunteers make a concerted effort to treat those who use their services as 'guests'. They can be a safe and welcoming place for those experiencing marginalisation (39). However, using them can also be a source of shame, with confusing and 'othering' operational processes (57). Regularly using food banks and similar services can leave people feeling powerless, scrutinised, and judged (58). Food banks can function as an extension of increasingly restrictive and stigmatising welfare landscapes which can lead to additional challenges for the vulnerable people who use then (59). On a more practical level, food banks can regularly run out of food and may be unable to meet the dietary needs of vulnerable populations (60).

Food banks have become both synonymous with food poverty (23) and a symbolic salve, serving as a moral safety valve as food poverty increases (61). In the years before national-level data on food poverty were routinely collected in the UK, food bank usage became an established proxy indicator of food poverty (16, 62). In particular, the prevalence and location of Trussell Trust food banks (the largest network of food banks in the UK) as a as a proxy measure for levels of food poverty and the extent of food aid provision. However, this approach, although pragmatic, is inherently problematic (50). It likely underestimates food poverty as only a proportion of food insecure households will access a food bank (63). Added to which, the franchise nature of food bank set ups means that the opening and location of food banks are based on community resources and the capacity of local social networks. Therefore, the absence of a food bank in a particular area does not necessarily equate to the absence of food poverty. The absence of a food bank in a deprived area could simply be due to a lack of local resource and volunteer-base (50). An alternative place-based approach to using food banks as a proxy is calculating household *food poverty risk* at the neighbourhood level. So rather than counting food banks and food parcels, it relies upon working out who is most at risk of food poverty and then mapping where groups of those people live. We did this by estimating the geographic distribution of factors contributing to household food poverty (such as the proportion of people claiming certain benefits and levels of benefit sanctions) (Ibid.)

## Food poverty and the right to food

In the UK, the stigma associated with receiving food aid is a barrier to accessing food banks (64). Food poverty is a social justice issue, bound-up with inequality and marginalisation. The right to food is a human right that protects the right of people to feed themselves in dignity (65). It is a right than many countries recognise (66), including the UK (67). A rights-based approach to food poverty recognises that wealthier countries often to not meet their obligations to protect, respect and fulfil people's right to food. Further, that the state does not sufficiently involve itself in efforts to address wider inequalities and the problems faced by those on low-incomes that lead to food poverty (29).

Campaigners for a 'Right to Food' argue for a *legal* right to food, placing responsibility on the Government to end hunger and prohibiting them from taking actions and implementing policies that result in increasing levels of food poverty and hardship (68). Food poverty is a political issue and the right to food cannot be separated from the right to health (29).

A rights-based approach takes a critical stance on charity, food banks, and the donation of surplus food. Charitable food aid, and especially food banking, is a moral and pragmatic response to persistent food poverty, but it also contains a self-interested or self-perpetuating quality (69). On the ground, food bank organisers and volunteers are very much aware of these tensions (70) and, in my experience, have divergent views on what food aid is there to do and how these tensions could or should be resolved. It is entirely possible, and probably quite common, to actively participate in the food banking system and, at the same time, hold deep reservations about the welfare policies and ideologies of governance that it is mitigating (Ibid). Appeals and mission statements to end the need for food banks are increasingly common within the food aid sector itself (namely the Trussell Trust and IFAN), as are calls for a 'cash first' approach to food poverty which aims to reduce the need for charitable food aid by helping people access existing financial entitlements and get advice on income maximisation (71, 72). To date, relatively little attention has been paid to the politics of the food bank providers and the charitable food aid system (59).

## Food poverty as a symptom and a sub-type

As previously stated, in wealthier countries, food scarcity is rarely the reason people go hungry. Therefore, if food poverty is not caused by a lack of food, and food poverty cannot (and has not) been solved by distributing surplus and donated food, then what does that mean for the way researchers think about and approach the issue? There is a long-standing framing of food poverty as a symptom of social ills and structural inequities, including inadequate welfare provision (73), stigmatising neoliberal ideology (74), and extreme inequality (75). Food poverty has been described as a symptom of a 'social disease' spreading across Western countries, one that is inseparable from social and health inequalities and their causes (76).

In our own research (39), we situated food poverty as a facet of 'advanced marginality' (77) and a result of structural barriers to full inclusion and citizenship. Further, we have argued that food poverty can be understood as a particular type of poverty. Poverty is about more than low incomes and it is not a uniform experience. Particular aspects of the experience of poverty have implications for diet and dietary health. It is increasingly apparent that *uncertainty* is one of those aspects (78). Specifically, chronic precarity around the social determinants of health (like housing and income) deprioritises diet and can make it extremely difficult, and sometimes impossible, to afford, store and prepare food (Ibid).

In addition to being indicative or symptomatic of wider problems and phenomena, food poverty is also, essentially, a subtype of poverty. As we saw in Chapter 2, the terms that we use to describe the various facets and experiences of poverty and deprivation have power. Food deserts is an emotive term that captured the attention of the public and policy makers. It provides an accessible metaphor for area-based problem with multiple and complex causes. Similarly, 'food poverty' is a powerful and widely used term that has both positive (for campaigning) and negative (does not necessarily capture the experience of hunger) connotations (79).

In recent years, discussion and identification of other 'types' of poverty have been theorised and applied to try and understand contemporary experiences of deprivation. Fuel poverty is now widely recognised in the UK as a distinct form of social inequality (80). The term period poverty refers to the inability of low-income women and girls in UK to afford period products, a condition that has been linked to gendered poverty and stigma (81). Transport poverty is household financial hardship resulting from transport costs (82). More recently, COVID-19 restrictions and the resulting necessity for remote-learning has highlighted digital poverty (83).

There are varied possible explanations for this proliferation of sub-types. It could be a function of neo-liberal ideology, depoliticising poverty (84) by breaking it down into discrete facets (79) and, thereby, obscuring broader structural inequalities. Focusing on individual sub-types of poverty gives the impression that there is just one issue that needs addressing isolation (85), like food or fuel. This new language of poverty positions the marginalised as a collection of needs and deficiencies rather than as human actors with fundamental rights (86).

Alternatively, it could be a discursive consequence of severe and widening inequalities. The sub-types are concepts that help us understand the increasingly harsh and varied experiences of extreme marginalisation. There has been a deepening and intensification of financial hardship for those on the lowest incomes, with the proportion of people falling below the poverty line growing since 2010 (87). Experiences such as living for months on end in temporary accommodation without access to a kitchen or being unable to afford enough fuel to get to work warrant attention and recognition and using sub-types of poverty to describe them is a way of doing that. Different sub-types of poverty can be understood as various 'spokes in the wheel of wider deprivation' (88).

However, while these terms might be useful conceptually and in terms of surveillance and measurement, people who experience hardship do not tend use them to describe their plight. In the course of my research, I have yet to encounter anyone who explained their use of a food bank in terms of food poverty. Sub-types of poverty are externally imposed concepts. A GP working in a deprived London Borough neatly summed it up by dismissing 'food poverty' as just 'poverty poverty' (70).

## Conclusion

Research on food poverty is a diverse and multi-disciplinary body of work. In the UK, the lack of national-level policy, intervention and sometimes even acknowledgement of the issue has meant that the research agenda on food poverty has been shaped and driven by the third sector organisations tackling (food) poverty and the academics who work closely with them. Innovative work has been done to map the extent and severity of food poverty and to characterise the food bank system. While it is crucial to understand the scale of the problem, it is fair to say that none of these measures, proxies, or estimations have produced unexpected findings. Food poverty tends to be more prevalent and severe in poorer areas. Food poverty increased as the incomes of some of the most vulnerable members of society were lowered by welfare reform. A pertinent example of this is the roll-out of Universal Credit, which was significantly associated with an increase in food bank use (16). This lends weight to the argument that food poverty in wealthier countries is preventable and the result of structural and economic inequalities. Despite this, potential policy solutions are largely directed towards individuals and households rather than at social determinants (29), leaving poorer households without relief from rising living costs and falling incomes and reliant on charitable food. Reliance on food aid should not be part of any modern society-wide and evidence-based approach to public policy (42).

# References

1. Craig G, Dowler E. Let them eat cake! poverty, hunger and the UK state. In: Riches G, editor. *First world hunger: food security and welfare politics.* University of Toronto Press; 1997. p. 108–33.
2. Lang T. Dividing up the cake: food as social exclusion. In: Walker A, Walker C, editors. *Britain divided.* CPAG; 1997.
3. Hawkes C, Webster J. *Too much and too little? debates of surplus food redistribution.* Sustain; 2000.
4. Riches G. Hunger and the welfare state: comparative perspectives. In: Riches G, editor. *First world hunger: food security and welfare politics.* University of Toronto Press; 1997. p. 1–13.
5. Tarasuk V. A critical examination of community-based responses to household food insecurity in Canada. *Health Education and Behavior.* 2001;28(4):478–99.
6. Sosenko F, Littlewood M, Bramley G, Fitzpatrick S, Blenkinsopp J, Wood J. *State of hunger: a study of poverty and food insecurity in the UK.* The Trussell Trust; 2019.
7. FAO, IFAD, UNICEF, WFP, WHO. *In brief to the state of food security and nutrition in the world 2020. Transforming food systems for affordable healthy diets.* ROME, Nations FaAOotU; 2020.
8. Poppendieck J. *Breadlines knee deep in wheat: food assistance in the great depression.* University of California Press; 2014.
9. Magdoff F. The world food crisis. *Monthly Review.* 2008;60(1):1–15.
10. Institute of M, National Research C. *Supplemental nutrition assistance program: examining the evidence to define benefit adequacy.* Julie AC, Ann LY, editors. The National Academies Press; 2013.
11. Global Food Security. *UK threat.* The Biotechnology and Biological Sciences Research Council (BBSRC). 2022.
12. *Number of hungry people rises to 963 million* [press release]. https://www.fao .org/resilience/news-events/detail/en/c/147940/2008.
13. Mittal A. The 2008 food price crisis: rethinking food security policies. In: United Nations Conference on Trade and Development; New York. 2009.
14. Fairclough I. Evaluating policy as argument: the public debate over the first UK austerity budget. *Critical Discourse Studies.* 2015;13(1):57–77.
15. Garthwaite KA, Collins PJ, Bambra C. Food for thought: an ethnographic study of negotiating ill health and food insecurity in a UK foodbank. *Social Science & Medicine.* 2015;132:38–44.
16. Jenkins RH, Aliabadi S, Vamos EP, Taylor-Robinson D, Wickham S, Millett C, et al. The relationship between austerity and food insecurity in the UK: a systematic review. *EClinicalMedicine.* 2021;33:100781.
17. Lambie-Mumford H. *Food bank provision and welfare reform in the UK.* SPERI: Sheffield Political Economy Research Institute; 2014.
18. Butler B. Welfare spending for UK's poorest shrinks by £37bn. *The Guardian.* 2018 23rd September 2018.
19. Congress TU. *Getting it right this time: lessons from a decade of failed austerity.* TUC; 2019.

20. Panjwani A, Reland J. *Employment: what's happened to wages since 2010*. Full Fact; 2019.

21. Joyce R. *Poverty and low pay in the UK: the state of play and the challenges ahead*. UKRI: Economic and Social Research Council; 2018 Available from: https://ifs.org.uk/publications/11696.

22. Cominetti N, McCurdy C, Slaughter H. *Low pay Britain*. Resolution Foundation. 2021.

23. Wells R, Caraher MUK. Print media coverage of the food bank phenomenon: from food welfare to food charity? *British Food Journal*. 2014;116:1426–45.

24. International Food Policy Research Institute. *Food security*. IFPRI; 2022 Available from: https://www.ifpri.org/topic/food-security#:~:text=Food%20security,%20as%20defined%20by,an%20active%20and%20healthy%20life.

25. Taylor A, Loopstra R. *Too poor to eat: food insecurity in the UK*. The Food Foundation; 2016.

26. Beacom E, Furey S, Hollywood L, Humphreys P. Investigating food insecurity measurement globally to inform practice locally: a rapid evidence review. *Critical Reviews in Food Science and Nutrition*. 2021;61(20):3319–39.

27. Dowler E. Food and poverty in Britain: rights and responsibilities. *Social Policy and Administration*. 2002;36(6):698–717.

28. Pinstrup-Andersen P. Food security: definition and measurement. *Food Security*. 2009;1:5–7.

29. Dowler E, O'Connor D. Rights-based approaches to addressing food poverty and food insecurity. *Social Science & Medicine*. 2012;74:44–51.

30. O'Connor N, Farag K, Baines R. What is food poverty? A conceptual framework. *British Food Journal*. 2015;118(2):429–49.

31. Garratt E. Please sir, I want some more: an exploration of repeat foodbank use. *BMC Public Health*. 2017;17(1):828–39.

32. The Trussell Trust. *End of year stats*. 2021. Available from: https://www.trusselltrust.org/news-and-blog/latest-stats/end-year-stats/.

33. Markovic TP, Natoli SJ. Paradoxical nutritional deficiency in overweight and obesity: the importance of nutrient density. *Medical Journal of Australia*. 2009;190(3):149–51.

34. Dinour LM, Bergen D, Yeh M. The food insecurity-obesity paradox: a review of the literature and the role food stamps may play. *Journal of the American Dietetic Association*. 2007;107(11):1952–61.

35. Angelopoulou MV, Shanti SD, Gonzalez CD, Love A, Chaffin J. Association of food insecurity with early childhood caries. *Journal of Public Health Dentistry*. 2019;79(2):102–8.

36. Hanson KL, Connor LM. Food insecurity and dietary quality in US adults and children: a systematic review. *American Journal of Clinical Nutrition*. 2014;100(2):684–92.

37. Raphael D. *Social determinants of health: Canadian perspectives*. Canadian Scholars' Press; 2009.

38. Pooler JA, Hartline-Grafton H, DeBor M, Sudore RL, Seligman HK. Food insecurity: a key social determinant of health for older adults. *Journal of the American Geriatrics Society*. 2019;67(3):421–4.

39. Thompson C, Smith S, Cummins S. Understanding the health and wellbeing challenges of the food banking system: a qualitative study of food bank users, providers and referrers in London. *Social Science & Medicine*. 2018;211:95–101.

40. Elgar FJ, Pickett W, Pförtner TK, Gariépy G, Gordon D, Georgiades K, Davison C, Hammami N, MacNeil AH, Azevedo Da Silva M, Melgar-Quiñonez HR. Relative food insecurity, mental health and wellbeing in 160 countries. *Social Science and Medicine*. 2021:268.

41. Douglas F, Machray K, Entwistle V. Health professionals' experiences and perspectives on food insecurity and long-term conditions: a qualitative investigation. *Health & Social Care in the Community*. 2020;28(2):404–13.

42. Ashton JR, Middleton J, Lang T. Open letter to Prime Minister David Cameron on food poverty in the UK. *Lancet*. 2014;383(9929):1631.

43. Taylor-Robinson D, Rougeaus E, Harrison D, Whitehead M, Barr B, Pearce A. The rise of food poverty in the UK. *BMJ*. 2013;347.

44. Loopstra R. Rising food bank use in the UK: sign of a new public health emergency? *Nutrition Bulletin*. 2018;43(1):53–60.

45. Hefferon C, Taylor C, Bennett D, Falconer C, Campbell M, Williams JG, et al. Priorities for the child public health response to the COVID-19 pandemic recovery in England. *Archives of Disease in Childhood*. 2021;106(106):533–8.

46. Coleman-Jensen A, Rabbitt MP, Gregory CA, Singh A. *Household food security in the United States in 2014*. United States Department of Agriculture. 2015.

47. Tarasuk V, McIntyre L. *Food insecurity in Canada*. The Canadian Encyclopedia; 2020. https://www.thecanadianencyclopedia.ca/en/article /food-insecurity-in-canada#:~:text=Measuring%20Food%20Insecurity &text=Although%20national%20surveys%20as%20early,Household%20 Food%20Security%20Survey%20Module.

48. Loopstra R, Reeves A, Tarasuk V. The rise of hunger among low-income households: an analysis of the risks of food insecurity between 2004 and 2016 in a population-based study of UK adults. *Journal of Epidemiology and Community Health*. 2019;73(7):668–73.

49. Loopstra R. *Measuring household food insecurity in the UK and why we MUST do it*. Food Foundation. 2017.

50. Smith D, Parker S, Harland K, Shelton N, Thompson C. Identifying populations and areas at greatest risk of household food insecurity in England. *Applied Geography*. 2018;91:21–31.

51. Department for Work and Pensions. *Family resources survey: financial year 2019 to 2020*. 2021. Available from: https://www.gov.uk/government /statistics/family-resources-survey-financial-year-2019-to-2020/family -resources-survey-financial-year-2019-to-2020#household-food-security-1.

52. Poppendieck J. *Sweet charity? Emergency food and the end of entitlement*. Penguin; 1998.

53. Lambie-Mumford H. 'Every town should have one': emergency food banking in the UK. *Journal of Social Policy*. 2013;42(1):73–89.

54. Lambie-Mumford H. The growth of food banks in Britain and what they mean for social policy. *Critical Social Policy* 2018;39(1):3–22.

55. Independent Food Aid Network. *Mapping the UK's independent food banks*. IFAN; 2020. Available from: https://www.foodaidnetwork.org.uk/ independent-food-banks-map.

56. Cloke P, May J, Williams A. The geographies of food banks in the meantime. *Progress in Human Geography*. 2016;41(6):703–26.

57. McNaughton D, Middleton G, Mehta K, Booth S. Food charity, shame/ing and the enactment of worth. *Medical Anthropology*. 2021;40(1):98–109.

58. Pemberton S, Fahmy E, Sutton E, Bell K. Endless pressure: life on a low income in Austere times. *Social Policy & Administration*. 2017;51:1156–73.

59. Williams A, Cloke P, May J. Contested space: the contradictory political dynamics of food banking in the UK. *Environment and Planning A*. 2016;48(11):2291–316.

60. Ronson D, Caraher M. Food banks: big society or shunting yards? Successful failures. In: Caraher M, Coveney J, editors. *Food poverty and insecurity: international food inequalities*. Springer International; 2016. p. 77–88.

61. Riches G. Food banks don't solve food poverty. The UK must not institutionalise them. *The Guardian*. 2014 Monday 8th December 2014.

62. Power M. *Proxy longitudinal indicators of household food insecurity in the UK*. Emerald Open Research. 2021.

63. Loopstra R, Tarasuk V. Food bank usage is a poor indicator of food insecurity: insights from Canada. *Social Policy & Society*. 2015;14(3):443–55.

64. Lambie-Mumford H, Crossley D, Jensen E, Verbeke M, Dowler E. *Household food security in the UK: a review of food aid*. Department for Environment, Food and Rural Affairs; 2014.

65. United Nations. *Special Rapporteur on the right to food: human rights*. Office of the High Commissioner; 2021. Available from: https://www.ohchr.org/en/issues/food/pages/foodindex.aspx.

66. Food and Agriculture Organization of the United States. *The right to food*. 2022. Available from: https://www.fao.org/right-to-food/en/.

67. Ferrando T, Dalmeny K. *A UK right to food law could tackle food poverty and environmental degradation*. University of Bristol; 2018.

68. Westwater H. What is the right to food? *The Big Issue*. 2021 25th June 2021.

69. Riches G. *Food bank nations: poverty, corporate charity and the right to food*. Routledge; 2018.

70. Thompson C, Smith DM, Cummins S. "We shouldn't need to be here": the perceived social goods and ills of foodbanks and food aid in London's changing welfare landscape. In: Royal Geographical Society RGS-IBG Annual International Conference; London; 2017.

71. Independent Food Aid Network. *The independent food aid network (IFAN) and a cash first approach to food insecurity*. 2020. Available from: https://www.foodaidnetwork.org.uk/cash-first.

72. Food Plymouth. *Vital resource for cash first approach to food insecurity in Plymouth*. 2021. Available from: https://foodplymouth.org/vital-resource-cash-first-leaflet-plymouth/#:~:text=The%20aim%20of%20a%20Cash,first%20response%20to%20food%20insecurity.

73. Cooper N, Purcell S, Jackson R. *Below the breadline: the relentless rise of food poverty in Britain*. Church Action on Poverty and Oxfam; 2014.

74. Swales S, May C, Nuxoll M, Tucker C. Neoliberalism, guilt, shame and stigma: a Lacanian discourse analysis of food insecurity. *Journal of Community & Applied Social Psychology.* 2020(30):673–87.

75. Garthwaite KA. *Hunger pains: life inside foodbank Britain.* Policy Press; 2016.

76. Roncarolo F, Potvin L. Food insecurity as a symptom of a social disease: analyzing a social problem from a medical perspective. *Canadian Family Physician.* 2016;62:291–2.

77. Wacquant L. Territorial stigmatization in the age of advanced marginality. *Thesis Eleven.* 2007;91(1):66–77.

78. Thompson C. Dietary health in the context of poverty and uncertainty around the social determinants of health. *Proceedings of the Nutrition Society.* 2021;(online ahead of print):1–14. https://www.cambridge.org/core/journals/proceedings-of-the-nutrition-society/article/dietary-health-in-the-context-of-poverty-and-uncertainty-around-the-social-determinants-of-health/D11F4A99870B9DE4AC7A92D2F376A263.

79. Spelling C. *Language matters, especially when it comes to achieving food justice* [Internet]. Sustain; 2021. Available from: https://www.sustainweb.org/blogs/jan21-language-matters-achieving-food-justice/.

80. Walker G, Simcock N, Day R. Necessary energy uses and a minimum standard of living in the United Kingdom: energy justice or escalating expectations? *Energy Research & Social Science.* 2016;18:129–38.

81. Briggs A. Period poverty'in Stoke-on-Trent, UK: new insights into gendered poverty and the lived experiences of austerity. *Journal of Poverty and Social Justice.* 2021;29(1):85–102.

82. Lucas K, Mattioli G, Verlinghieri E, Guzman A. Transport poverty and its adverse social consequences. *Proceedings of the Institution of Civil Engineers: Transport.* 2016;169:353–65.

83. Donaghy D. Defining digital capital and digital poverty. *ITNOW.* 2021;63(1):54–5.

84. Lyon-Callo V, Hyatt SB. The neoliberal state and the depoliticization of poverty: activist anthropology and "ethnography from below. *Urban Anthropology and Studies of Cultural Systems and World Economic Development.* 2003;32(2):175–204.

85. Rayner J. Don't talk about 'food poverty' – it's just poverty. *The Guardian.* 2019 16th May 2019.

86. Chakrabortty A. The problem is poverty, however we label it. *The Guardian.* 2021 21st January 2021.

87. Edmiston D. Plumbing the Depths: the changing (socio-demographic) profile of UK poverty. *Journal of Social Policy.* 2021:1–27. https://eprints.whiterose.ac.uk/170704/.

88. Chapman S. Food poverty and fuel poverty go hand in hand. *The New Statesman.* 2016 26th February 2022.

# 4 New geographies of food access and inequality

## Research context and aims

We recognise the competing priorities between academic research, where outputs are peer reviewed publications and contributions to the evidence-base for government or policy. This is in contrast with the needs of civil society to measure impact of their activities, or for local government and policy makers who are tasked with choosing which intervention approach to follow to reduce population health inequalities in food access and diet quality. Often, local government in the UK has the unenviable task of deciding how to allocate increasingly limited and sometimes ring-fenced funds to support interventions to reduce food insecurity. They need to identify the most appropriate investment for maximum return.

At the applied end of the research spectrum, studies conducted either by civil society, public sector actors, academics, or a combination of all three, tend – by necessity – to have a fairly limited range of aims. Invariably, these include variations on one or more of the following:

1) Understanding the current food insecurity situation for a discrete area or population.
2) Identifying how food insecurity can be addressed and devising interventions to action this.
3) Evaluating, through process evaluations and impact evaluations, to find out: whether interventions and policies have actually eased food insecurity; who they have worked for; and if they are sustainable over the longer term.

Essentially, applied research at a local level tends to be concerned with finding out: the extent of food insecurity in a given area; identifying actions (interventions) that could help; and then assessing if those interventions work. As previously discussed, such endeavours are often

DOI: 10.4324/9781003184560-4

necessarily pragmatic and reactive undertakings because the main drivers of food insecurity are national level policies and trends that are outside of the control of the local actors who are tasked with responding to it. Local-level research, therefore, has two main areas of concern (Table 4.1):

- **Stressors** that drive and exacerbate food insecurity locally (some of which overlap with national drivers)
- Place-based **resources and facilitators** – including existing interventions – that can be harnessed to mitigate food insecurity

*Table 4.1* Relationships between research aims, characteristics, and outcomes

| | | Stressors (local) | Place-based resources and facilitators | Research examples |
|---|---|---|---|---|
| **Research aim:** | Understanding the extent of food insecurity for a given area | ● | | – Needs assessments<br>– Defining the local food environment<br>– Food basket comparisons<br>– Estimating food insecurity risk |
| | Identifying actions (interventions) that could help | | ● | – Mapping the food aid environment<br>– Strategic place-based agreements (like Food Poverty Action Plans) |
| | Evaluating those interventions to find out if they work | ● | ● | – Impact evaluation<br>– Process evaluation<br>Getting feedback from service users and stakeholders |

In this chapter, we present a new framework for data collection and analysis – based on various attempts and experiences of trying to address these research aims. We stress that this framework is relevant to research about understanding, addressing, and mitigating food insecurity. It is not about preventing or even ending food insecurity. That could only be achieved by addressing national level drivers such as income poverty, widening inequality, reduced welfare provision, and regressive taxation (1).

## Theoretical frameworks for Social Determinants of Health

Inherently, food and diet are social determinants of health (SDH) (2). The social determinants of health are the conditions and environments in which people are born, grow, age, work, and live. The quality of these resources and our access to them has a direct impact on our health outcomes. Unsurprisingly, access and quality tend to be better in higher income neighbourhoods – as discussed at length in the description of food deserts in Chapter 2. Access to food, especially nutritious food, has a direct impact on wellbeing, physical, and mental health. Research and interventions that address food insecurity are now at the forefront of strategies to address the social determinants of health (3). The conditions under which people live, especially their income, housing, and local food environment, shape their access to nutritious food and dictate the range of food choices they can make (4).

Social determinants of health, like welfare provision, are modifiable, and so can be improved or refined. Up-stream, or structural, public health interventions seek to do just this: to improve the quality, distribution of, or access to one or some of the social determinants of health for particular groups and populations. The World Health Organisation (WHO), in their final report of the Commission on Social Determinants of Health, outlined three points of action in this theme: 1) Improve daily living conditions; 2) Tackle the inequitable distribution of power, money and resources; and 3) Measure and understand the problem and assess the impact of action (5). The second point – tackling structural inequality – is largely beyond the scope of local-level interventions and the research that informs them. The first and third, however, improving conditions and measuring the problem, can be undertaken at the local level. In fact, measurement is essential if local government is to make the best of use of the limited funds it has available to mitigate inequalities in food access.

The Dahlgren and Whitehead model of the social determinants describes the range of influences on health with individual characteristics at the centre (6). In this model, individual lifestyle factors (like physical activity, diet, and smoking) are choices constrained by wider economic and social circumstances. While some might be regarded as 'free choice' – people can choose whether or not smoke, for example – others are not. Notably, the extent to which diet quality can be thought of as an outcome of individual and personal choices is limited. People's food choices, and therefore their diet quality, are constrained by factors such their personal and community networks and, more broadly, by income and the quality of the local food environment. The most distal (outer) layer of influences in this model acknowledges the general cultural and socioeconomic conditions of a place.

These include factors like taxation and the availability of paid work opportunities (7). What is not clearly present in this model is the political environment, such as policies that would address health inequalities influenced by the social determinants of health. As discussed in Chapter 3, (food) poverty is a political issue and, by association, research and interventions around food insecurity can be politically sensitive (8) – as we will explore further in Chapter 5.

Krieger's ecosocial theory incorporates life course, political economy, and geographic scale (9) more effectively than the Dahlgren and Whitehead model. This model explains causal relationships in disease distribution over the life course with reference to biological, psychosocial, and social factors. A life course approach can entail theorising the cumulative effects of disadvantaged circumstances on health (10). Life course approaches can also involve looking at situations that will impact on health outcomes at critical points of human development. A useful example of this is the Developmental Origins of Health and Disease [DOHAD] theory which grew from early work by David Barker (11). The DOHAD theory is based on the concept that the origins of lifestyle related conditions and disease are formed at the time of fertilization, embryonic, foetal, and neonatal stages of development by the interrelation between genes and the environment (specifically nutrition, stress, and environmental chemicals). DOHAD links the state of health and risk from disease in childhood and adult life with those environmental conditions of early life and development (12). Life course effects are crucial to include in studies of health inequalities, and particularly around inequalities in food access.

The ANGELO framework (Analysis Grid for Environments Linked to Obesity) takes a place-based, rather than life course, approach to the social determinants of health. It categorises the social and environmental drivers of diet across four domains: physical, economic, legislative, and socio-cultural (13). The framework provides a conceptual model for understanding the obesogenicity of environments and, thereby, serves as a tool for prioritising elements of those environments for research and intervention (14). An obesogenic environment is one in which obesity is a normal response to a pathological environment, specifically one that promotes obesity in individuals or populations (15).

The ANGELO framework has been widely used for planning appropriate policy by addressing differing leverage points across these themed areas as well as the micro and macro environments (16). The utility of the ANGELO approach is the ease with which areas and populations can be broadly described and opportunities for improving environments identified. An example of a macro-level intervention, one that operates at the scale of the political environment, would be the introduction of the sugar tax in the UK (https://www.gov.uk/government/news/soft-drinks-industry -levy-comes-into-effect). Our focus is more on the micro-level environments of neighbourhoods or even schools, as this is where local governments have authority to enact changes. One example of a micro-level intervention would be the opening of a food aid service such as a food bank or pantry.

Each of the social determinants of health frameworks described above includes the influential roles of place and personal characteristics, which are crucial to any research in health inequalities (17). The influence of place on individual health behaviours and outcomes is also mediated by individual or household level characteristics. For instance, a person living in an area with higher rates of crime will be less affected by the risk of crime if they can pay to put an alarm on their house, keep their car in a garage or live in a gated property. If someone living in the same area cannot pay for additional security, then they will experience a greater impact of living in an area with higher crime. A similar analogy would be whether someone can afford sufficient heating in a cold climate; people who are economically disadvantaged are less able to buffer themselves against negative aspects of their living environment.

Macintyre and colleagues called this scenario 'deprivation amplification' and extended it to explain how policy can address both area and individual-level influences to ameliorate health inequalities (18). Macintyre takes a critical view of this theory from the perspective that socially deprived areas may not always lack resources, which would compound individual material deprivation (e.g., poorer areas have fewer supermarkets where food is affordable, or quality green space for exercise). However, we suggest that the consideration of deprivation amplification can add value to local-level studies on food insecurity. What may be useful is to remove 'deprivation' from the descriptor of an area and look at it from a resource or asset perspective, as we outline in Chapter 5. In other words, what is present in a location which may facilitate improvements and mitigation for people who are experiencing food insecurity or who are at risk of food insecurity?

Overall, to understand food insecurity we need to look at places people live, characterise the factors that influence their food access and diet quality, and ascertain if they need to use food aid to achieve a diet of reasonable quality. Together, these considerations can be used to develop area profiles of food insecurity.

## Area-based interventions and studies

The 2010 Marmot Review explicitly called for healthier and sustainable communities, supporting the drive to make positive changes to infrastructure and resources (19). This place-based focus is reflective of the early 2000s public policy trend in the UK, and across Western Europe more generally, to shift the focus and responsibility for health away from individuals, and instead to consider the ways in which areas and neighbourhoods could be changed to better support the health of populations (20). Pertinent examples of this include: the Mind, Exercise, Nutrition, Do It! (MEND) study which was focused on children and their families and, although not universally available, had some success, (21) and the Healthy Towns initiative, which we explore below.

Between 2008 and 2011, Public Health England set out funding to support area-based interventions in cities with the express purpose of supporting community-led interventions to reduce population obesity. This was referred to as the Healthy Towns initiative (Healthy Community Challenge Fund) (22). These funds allocated money to nine towns, with the instruction to develop a 'locality-specific programme of interventions' to address obesogenic environments. Local authorities and Primary Care Trusts were invited to bid jointly for funding, with a limit of £5 million per town, which they had to match-fund from local sources and partners. Towns were expected to deliver a coherent multi-sector plan that implemented a programme of interventions in their local area that suited their particular situation (23). This is certainly preferable to rolling out a generic intervention programme without considering the population characteristics. For example, it would be less useful to devise a programme to encourage cycling where there is no road infrastructure to make it safe. The programme generated more than 300 local interventions around physical activity, active travel, growing, and urban planning (22).

As a condition of the funding these sites all had to undertake evaluations of their 'locally specific' interventions to assess the impact of what was developed and also to understand the challenges (and successes) of the process required to implement them. This was achieved through a combination of local process and impact evaluations and a wider evaluation of the development and implementation of the programme itself (22). A process evaluation determines whether the intervention activities were implemented as intended, what barriers were encountered, what changes are needed, and why outcomes were or were not achieved (24). An impact evaluation is an assessment of how the intervention affects health outcomes and whether these effects were intended or unintended. In short, it ascertains the degree to which the intervention was successful (25). The combination of impact and process evaluations is ideal when assessing value for money of funded projects, and is aligned with the third WHO recommendation, as noted previously, for addressing inequalities related to the social determinants of health (measuring the problem and assessing the impact of actions to address it (5)).

Place-based and whole system approaches to addressing obesity have become increasingly popular and well documented, even if evidence of how to operationalise them is still in its infancy (26). Identifying and studying locality-based approaches to food insecurity, by comparison, is less straightforward. In wealthier countries, food insecurity (or food poverty) is a subtype of poverty and strongly predicated on income poverty and deprivation. Therefore, interventions to reduce and mitigate income deprivation, via cash transfers and increasing financial income, might reasonably be assumed to also reduce food insecurity. However, very few studies have evaluated their impact on food insecurity (27).

In the UK context, this is compounded by the fact that national measures of food insecurity have only recently been introduced by government, so it has simply not been possible to robustly evaluate the impact of interventions to reduce it without incorporating a direct measure of food insecurity or food insecurity outcomes in the study design, or relying on proxy measures instead. Without adequate measures of both insecurity and impact from interventions, it is impossible to evaluate whether initiative meet their own aims or address the growing problem of food insecurity (28).

Food banks are the dominant response to food insecurity in many wealthier countries, especially the UK, and yet there remains an absence of well-designed evaluations of their effectiveness (27). There is a similar lack of evidence around other local food initiatives, such as community kitchens (Ibid). This lack of evidence extends beyond food insecurity outcomes and into health outcomes more generally (29). Interventions may be set up without a theoretical framework that supports impact evaluation, and this can certainly be the case with many charitable food aid interventions which grow from the determination of one person or group to help others. Because health often takes time to change, there is also the simple challenge of time itself and following up with people to identify what, if any impact, an intervention such as food aid may have on their health.

In terms of strategic place-based food insecurity interventions in the UK, food poverty action plans (FPAPs) have become the de facto model (30). Food Poverty Action Plans (FPAPs) are community-level food insecurity interventions (31). They are locally agreed strategies for tackling food insecurity for a period of 2–4 years, after which a new plan is agreed. They aim to improve access to nutritious food for disadvantaged groups and address the drivers of food insecurity by increasing access to services such as food banks, cooking classes, debt and welfare benefits advice, and infant feeding support. Effectively, their intention is to address food poverty by providing support around the social determinants of health, with a focus on food access. FPAPs are often led by local authorities and supported by local multi-sector alliances (or networks). FPAPs are a place-based approach.

As such, there is variation in how they are delivered, the range of drivers addressed, and the diversity of stakeholders involved (32). We are not aware of any efforts to collate the different permutations of FPAPs. Despite first being piloted in 2013, FPAPs have not been robustly evaluated for their potential to reduce food insecurity or improve health outcomes. As will be covered in Chapter 5, we have worked extensively with local authorities to support FPAPs.

## New conceptual framework to support place-based research on food insecurity

The situation remains in the UK and in the US that national policies are not in place to adequately address, much less eradicate, food insecurity. What is feasible in local areas is to study the circumstances that people live in with a view to understanding the extent of food insecurity, the drivers of this insecurity, and what solutions are in place to help people who are unable to have a diet of sufficient quality – ideally without resorting to food aid. To support this type of locally focused research we have developed a conceptual framework that can be applied, influenced by the ANGELO framework, to consider points for data collection and intervention. Together this can help those working to understand food insecurity in communities as they address local and national calls for action. We also outline how impact and process can be measured, to help determine the most appropriate interventions for a particular place or population.

In order to do this, we return the two main areas of concern for applied local-level food insecurity research:

- **Stressors** that drive and exacerbate inequality locally
- Place-based **resources and facilitators** (including existing food insecurity interventions)

The division of influences into stressors and resources and facilitators reflects the competing situations in communities. As we have already discussed, the drivers of food insecurity are well established, largely the result of national-level policies, and fundamentally income-based. However, these overarching causes can be exacerbated by local place-based **stressors**. To illustrate, the distribution of food aid outlets across the UK can me understood in terms of capacity as much as it can in terms of 'need' (33). There are simply some places in which organising efforts to address food insecurity is more difficult. Currently, there is an uneven geography of responses to food insecurity in rural and coastal areas (34). Transport (especially a lack of public transport), for example, can have a disproportionate impact on food insecurity in rural areas and leave those without a car unable to travel to secure sufficient food for their household. Similarly, food banks operating in rural areas face additional challenges as they often need to organise deliveries to service users and can find it difficult to identify those in need over the large geographic areas they may support. This became particularly evident during the pandemic, when food aid services were severely stretched (35). Therefore, limited transport options and rural settings can be understood as local place-based stressors in that they serve to exacerbate the impacts of income inequality and make it difficult to deliver services to mitigate them.

Equally, in coastal areas, seasonal declines in work opportunities and geographically isolated locations can amplify the challenges of food insecurity related to unemployment. The drivers of food insecurity may be well known, but the local stressors around these (Figure 4.1) must be explored by researchers working at the community level. The extent to which the various social determinants of health shape health outcomes and the ways in which those determinants are experienced is shaped by place, both at the local and national scale (36). Uncertainty and precarity around the social determinants of health are exacerbated by factors at the local level, such as housing shortages or changes to the local food environment (4).

We acknowledge that much of what is included in the **resources and facilitators** category (shown in Figure 4.1) is on the boundary of 'socially acceptable' as it includes free or very discounted food (from food banks and a variety of other types of organisations). As previously stated, this is a pragmatic approach. We are fundamentally opposed to policies that create and perpetuate the severe inequality and marginalisation that leads to food insecurity, and to the state retreat that creates the need for charitable food aid and leaves some low-income people dependent upon it. Whether we like it or not, food aid (largely in the form of charitable food provision), and in particular food banks, comprise some of the most significant and well-organised local-level resources through which food insecurity can be understood and addressed (37). Food aid organisers are also, typically, some of the most committed and engaged local partners that researchers could hope to work with. Food-focused civil society organisations, in particular The Trussell Trust, Sustain, and the Independent Food Aid Network (IFAN), have been vitally important, providing direct food aid and supporting interventions which maximise income and thereby improve household food security is an area of particular focus. However, the fact remains that when people go to a food bank, it's more likely to be money they need – not food (38).

We also recognise that food aid is an inherently inadequate response to food insecurity. Food banks, for example, need to have space and volunteers

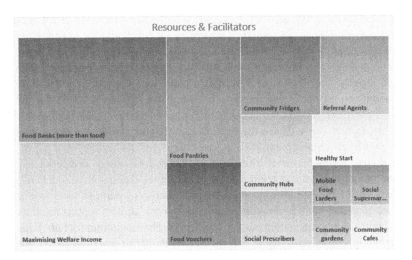

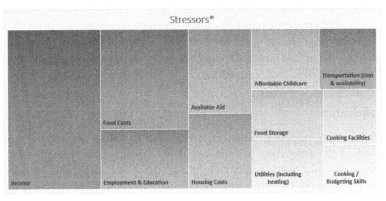

* 5-10% inflationary cost to most of these 'stressors'

*Figure 4.1* Conceptual framework for local food insecurity research.

to offer their services, so the areas where they are needed the most may not always have the capacity to support one. This can lead to greater inequalities for populations who lack the third sector resources which have been the primary response to food inequality in the UK, leading to a postcode lottery of help (39). This can mirror the situation of deprivation amplification where people living in more disadvantaged areas are facing limited personal and local resources that could improve their situation. With this substantial caveat acknowledged, we point to the work of Megan Blake, who frames community level resources and facilitators for mitigating food insecurity in terms of 'food ladders'. This is an evidenced-based approach to local-level resilience to food insecurity. Rather than focusing on the lack of food available to households it advocates for building place-specific levels of support that enable the recognition and enhancement of locally based skills and assets; and creating safe and inclusive spaces for interaction with and around food. Food ladders takes a place-based approach to capacity building to support those in crisis (utilising services like food banks and food pantries), and to facilitating community change via local food-related schemes that can increase the availability of food, build food skills, and even provide employment (40).

Local resources and infrastructure to address food insecurity: In our model there are a combination of proximal facilitators (food banks and vouchers, community fridges, food larders, pantries and social supermarkets; community cafes) and more distal support options (welfare support for income maximisation, social prescribers, community hubs) that encourage more sustainable action in households to improve their food security including nutritional quality.

Non-spatial: There are also online resources to provide tips on best use of food, cooking techniques and shopping/budgeting strategies that are not included as they are not in the physical space. Further facilitators are social networks where food and other resources can be shared, for example shared childcare to enable people to work.

## Conclusion

Urbanisation, persistent financial crises, and widening inequalities are changing the geography of food insecurity. Further, the combination of new governance mechanisms and state retreat have brought civil society into the food policy arena and are driving a new-localism around food inequality (41). In terms of income and health inequalities more broadly, the emphasis on localism after 2010 has devolved responsibility down to local areas to address health inequalities as they prioritise them (42). However, some action is being take at national levels to address income inequality. The most recent example of this is a pilot scheme in Wales to provide care leavers with a basic income, regardless of whether they are in work (43). A similar approach to income support was present during part of the COVID pandemic in 2020–2021 when people receiving Universal Credit were given a £20 a week uplift (one per household) to help them during this most difficult period. The impact of that added uplift ending was greater demand for food aid, demonstrating the direct link between income and food security in lower income households (44). This lends weight to the argument, and could even be seen as a partial acknowledgment of the fact, that food inequality should not be the responsibility of charities and local governments to 'solve' without wider state support and action.

Evaluations of what has worked (in terms of practicalities or health outcomes) can offer evidence of what helped to achieve the desired outcomes that can be used in other settings. Crucially, there needs to be a clear plan from the outset of the intervention to collect data that will enable some before and after comparison of population outcomes. Many area-based interventions are difficult to describe as successful partly because the outcome they address, such as obesity, is caused by many influences. Food insecurity, as is evident from existing research, needs to be addressed via the social determinants of health at the local and national level (45). It is difficult to prioritise what is not easily or regularly measured, and the food insecurity data collected as part of the Family Resource Survey cannot be mapped below the level of regions in the UK (of which there are nine), making it of limited use to local research.

Our proposed framework revises the layers of influence upon food insecurity and separates them into what supports (resources and facilitators) efforts to mitigate it and which place-based stressors can tip those already on very low incomes into extreme deprivation resulting in food insecurity. By extending the focus to explore social as well as physical environments, at a range of scales from household, neighbourhood, local district and country, the framework enables researchers to choose whether they concentrate on one aspect/level or also acknowledge the upstream drivers of food inequality. The framework is malleable and open to appropriate local modification, to support new research on or evaluations of interventions. This framework can complement individually focused interventions such as recommendations on diet from a medical professional or gym memberships. In Chapter 5 we describe these two approaches to interventions to illustrate their complex nature, which can make it difficult to measure impact.

## References

1. Riches G. *Independent food aid network*. 2019. Available from: https://www .foodaidnetwork.org.uk/blog/professor-graham-riches-on-exiting-us-style -corporate-food-banking-why-the.
2. Darmon N, Drewnowski A. Does social class predict diet quality? *American Journal of Clinical Nutrition*. 2008;87(5):1107–17.
3. Heath S. *How food security programs target social determinants of health: xtelligent healthcare media*. 2019. Available from: https://pat ientengagementhit.com/news/how-food-security-programs-target-social

-determinants-of-health#:~:text=Access%20to%20food%20%E2%80%93
%20nutritious%20food,illnesses%20they%20may%20already%20have.

4.   Thompson C. Dietary health in the context of poverty and uncertainty around
     the social determinants of health. *Proceedings of the Nutrition Society.*
     2021;(online ahead of print):1–14. https://www.cambridge.org/core/journals/
     proceedings-of-the-nutrition-society/article/dietary-health-in-the-context-
     of-poverty-and-uncertainty-around-the-social-determinants-of-health/
     D11F4A99870B9DE4AC7A92D2F376A263.

5.   World Health Organization. *Closing the gap in a generation: health equity
     through action on the social determinants of health - Final report of the
     commission on social determinants of health.* World Health Organization; 2008.

6.   Dahlgren G, Whitehead M. *Policies and strategies to promote social equity in
     health. Background document to WHO-Strategy paper for Europe.* Institute
     for Futures Studies; 1991.

7.   Public Health England. Chapter 6: Social determinants of health. In: *Health
     profile for England.* PHE (Public Health England) for the editor; 2017.

8.   Godrich SL, Barbour L, Lindberg R. Problems, policy and politics:
     perspectives of public health leaders on food insecurity and human rights in
     Australia. *BMC Public Health.* 2021;21.

9.   Krieger N. *Epidemiology and the people's health: theory and context.* Oxford
     University Press; 2011.

10.  Ben-Shlomo Y, Kuh D. A life course approach to chronic disease
     epidemiology: conceptual models, empirical challenges and interdisciplinary
     perspectives. Oxford University Press; 2002. p. 285–93.

11.  Barker D, Winter P, Osmond C, Margetts B, Simmonds S. Weight in infancy
     and death from ischaemic heart disease. *Lancet.* 1989;2(8663):577–580. Find
     this article online.

12.  Gluckman PD, Buklijas T, Hanson MA. Chapter 1: The developmental
     origins of health and disease (DOHaD) concept: past, present, and future. In:
     Rosenfeld CS, editor. *The epigenome and developmental origins of health
     and disease.* Academic Press; 2016. p. 1–15.

13.  Mooney JD, Jepson R, Frank J, Geddes R. Obesity prevention in
     scotland: a policy analysis using the ANGELO framework. *Obesity Facts.*
     2015;8:273–81.

14.  Swinburn B, Egger G, Raza F. Dissecting obesogenic environments:
     the development and application of a framework for identifying and
     prioritizing environmental interventions for obesity. *Preventative Medicine.*
     1999;29(6):563–70.

15.  Swinburn B, Egger G. Preventive strategies against weight gain and obesity.
     *Obesity Reviews.* 2002;3(4):289–301.

16.  Simmons A, Mavoa HM, Bell AC, De Courten M, Schaaf D, Schultz J, et al.
     Creating community action plans for obesity prevention using the ANGELO
     (analysis grid for elements linked to obesity) framework. *Health Promotion
     International.* 2009;24(4):311–24.

17. Macintyre S, Maciver S, Sooman A. Area, class and health: should we be focusing on places or people? *Journal of Social Policy.* 1993;22(2):213–34.

18. Macintyre S. Deprivation amplification revisited; or, is it always true that poorer places have poorer access to resources for healthy diets and physical activity? *International Journal of Behavioral Nutrition and Physical Activity.* 2007;4(1):32.

19. Marmot M, Goldblatt P, Allen J. Fair society, healthy lives. 2010. Strategic Review of Health Inequalities in England post-2010.

20. Van Gent W, Musterd S, Ostendorf W. Disentangling neighbourhood problems: area-based interventions in Western European cities. *Urban Research and Practice.* 2009;7(2):53–67.

21. Sacher PM, Kolotourou M, Chadwick PM, Cole TJ, Lawson MS, Lucas A, et al. Randomized controlled trial of the MEND program: a family-based community intervention for childhood obesity. *Obesity.* 2010;18(S1):S62–S8.

22. Cummins S, Ogilvie D, White M, Petticrew M, Jones A, Goodwin D, et al. *Challenge fund.* The Healthy Towns Programme in England; 2016.

23. Sautkina E, Goodwin D, Jones A, Ogilvie D, Petticrew M, White M, et al. Lost in translation? Theory, policy and practice in systems-based environmental approaches to obesity prevention in the Healthy Towns programme in England. *Health & Place.* 2014;29:60–6.

24. Linnan L, Steckler A. Process evaluation for public health interventions and research: an overview. In: Steckler A, Linnan L, editors. *Process evaluation for public health interventions and research.* Wiley; 2002.

25. Rogers P. *Overview of impact evaluation: methodological briefs: impact evaluation no. 1, methodological briefs no. 1.* Unicef; 2014.

26. Bagnall A-M, Radley D, Jones R, Gately P, Nobles J, Van Dijk M, et al. Whole systems approaches to obesity and other complex public health challenges: a systematic review. *BMC Public Health.* 2019;19(1):8.

27. Loopstra R. Interventions to address household food insecurity in high-income countries. *Proceedings of the Nutrition Society.* 2018;77(3):270–81.

28. Lambie-Mumford H, Sims L. "Feeding Hungry Children": the growth of charitable breakfast clubs and holiday hunger projects in the UK. *Children and Society.* 2018;32(3):244–54.

29. Aceves-Martins M, Cruickshank M, Fraser C, Brazzelli M. Child food insecurity in the UK: a rapid review. *Public Health Research.* 2018;6(13): 1–186.

30. Sustain. *Developing food poverty action plans.* Esmée Fairbairn Foundation, Trust for London and Sustainable Food Cities; 2016. https://www.london.gov .uk/sites/default/files/foodpovertyactionplans_shortguide.pdf.

31. Thompson C, Smith D, Cummins C, Argyropoulos E, Style H, Junaid A, et al. The challenges of local responses to food poverty in London: a summary of seminar discussions and presentations. PHI LAB: Supported by the Wellcome Trust. 2018. https://philab.lshtm.ac.uk/reports/.

32. NHS. *Place based approaches for addressing health inequalities.* 2019. Available from: https://www.england.nhs.uk/ltphimenu/placed-based -approaches-to-reducing-health-inequalities/place-based-approaches-for -reducing-health-inequalities/.

33. Smith D, Parker S, Harland K, Shelton N, Thompson C. Identifying populations and areas at greatest risk of household food insecurity in England. *Applied Geography.* 2018;91:21–31.

34. May J, Williams A, Cloke P, Cherry L. Still bleeding: The variegated geographies of austerity and food banking in rural England and Wales. *Journal of Rural Studies.* 2020;79:409–24.

35. Thompson C, Hamilton L, Dickinson A, Fallaize R, Mathie M, Rogers S, et al. *The impact of Covid-19 and the resulting mitigation measures on food and eating in the East of England: interim report.* NIHR ARC East of England and University of Hertfordshire; 2020.

36. De Maio F, Mazzeo J, Ritchie D. Social determinants of health: A view on theory and measurement. *Rhode Island Medical Journal.* 2013;1(96):15–9.

37. Williams A, Cloke P, May J, Goodwin M. Contested space: The contradictory political dynamics of food banking in the UK. *Environment and Planning A.* 2016;48(11):2291–316.

38. Goodwin S. *Report on Scotland's independent food banks: A menu for change.* Independent Food Aid Network; 2018.

39. Smith DM. *Mayors fund for London.* editor 2020. Available from: https:// www.mayorsfundforlondon.org.uk/wp-content/uploads/2020/05/Mayors -Fund_Digital-Digest-4_Dianna-Smith-Southampton-University.pdf.

40. Blake M. *Food ladders: A multi-scaled approach to everyday food security and community resilience.* University of Sheffield, ESTC, MRC, N8 AgriFood Programme; 2019.

41. Sonnino R. The new geography of food security: exploring the potential of urban food strategies. *The Geographical Journal.* 2014;182(2):190–200.

42. Regan P. Critical issues in practice development: localism and public health reforms. *Community Practitioner.* 2011;84(3):32–5.

43. BBC. *Basic income: Wales pilot offers £1,600 a month to care leavers.* BBC; 2022 [16th February 2022: Available from: https://www.bbc.co.uk/news/uk -wales-politics-60391462.

44. Disability Rights UK. *1.2 million UC claimants 'very likely' to turn to food banks if £20 a week uplift removed.* Disability Rights UK; 2021.

45. Thomson H. A dose of realism for healthy urban policy: lessons from area-based initiatives in the UK. *J Epidemiol Community Health.* 2008;62(10):932–6.

# 5 Food in place

## Methodological approaches to understanding inequalities in food

### Where is the food, and where are the people?

We begin by explaining the key questions posed for research studying food inequalities in places (as touched upon in Chapter 4) and work through the resources readily available to answer aspects of these questions. Throughout this chapter we are bringing in our research experience in localities across England. In some instances, we have formally consulted with partners to gather evidence on local challenges and support strategies developed as Food Poverty Action Plans. We focus on the framework set out in Chapter 4 to bring together two broad types of data collection, quantitative and qualitative (and crucially, where they overlap) while thinking about these data in terms of i) local stressors and ii) resources and facilitators to food equity. Much of our proposed approach takes an asset-based approach (like Blakes', which we discussed in Chapter 4) to evaluate resources, which we have found to be beneficial.

Arguably, the ideal starting point for place-based research is to assess the prevalence of diet-related health outcomes in small areas, then to work backwards to understand what is leading to poorer health in some populations. However, even in the UK where there is a national healthcare system, such localised data are not easily available. For this reason, we often rely upon proxy indicators or associated health outcomes. As we see in the food desert literature, child and adult obesity prevalence is one of the most common measures. Within the food insecurity literature poor mental health is another focal point (1). With both obesity and mental health, these outcomes are multifactorial, meaning that they are the result of several influences, and it can be difficult to disentangle where food insecurity (due to economic constraints, physical access, or other reasons) contributes to these outcomes. Poor health is a key driver of and justification for food insecurity research. Arguably, this is a result of researchers making a compelling case for funds to support their work on the grounds of public health. Food

DOI: 10.4324/9781003184560-5

insecurity is also within the remit of local authority public health teams who have to make evidence-based decisions on how to use their often-limited resources to support local services (as often food banks and similar community organisations can be funded, in part, by local government public health money).

## Qualitative data

Qualitative data – that which is generated by speaking to people who have experienced food insecurity and the professionals and volunteers who support them – has been instrumental in raising awareness about the issue and understanding the crises and pressures that tip people into food insecurity. Qualitative approaches produce narrative evidence about complex and context-specific issues using the accounts of those actively involved in them. As discussed in Chapter 4, while the drivers of food insecurity tend to be national, the local stressors and manifestations of this are highly situated. The local authorities and councils that we have worked with find qualitative data easy to understand (especially for non-specialists) and accessible. Qualitative accounts of food insecurity are powerful, as evidenced by the extent to which they feature in campaigning and fundraising around the issue by charities and other third sector organisations, such as Sustain and the Food Foundation.

## Lived experience

In recent years, there has been increased academic interest in the lived experience of food insecurity (2) and increased involvement of those with lived experience in campaigning and generating policy solutions (3). The term 'lived experience' can be a little problematic. Isn't all experience 'lived'? What other kinds of experience are there? While there are interesting theoretical debates and critiques about how the concept has evolved and the implications of using it (4), in terms of applied research a useful working definition is talking to and working with people who have direct experience of food insecurity (as opposed to those who may just have opinions on it and/or who have studied it). When conducting local needs assessments, it is common practice (and good practice) for researchers working with or for local authorities to conduct qualitative interviews with those who have lived experience of food insecurity and who have used food aid services. The advantages of this are clear, researchers can ask specific questions about local services and problems and can feedback on a range of issues.

However, interviewing people with lived experience of food insecurity can be very problematic both ethically and practically. It is difficult to recruit people experiencing food insecurity. They are, by definition, having considerable difficulties and probably experiencing significant marginalisation. The charities and volunteers who support them are, understandably, reluctant to introduce or pass on contact details to researchers. Even if they do, they are not necessarily going to want to talk to a stranger about difficult and potentially painful parts of their life. As previously discussed, the stigma around food insecurity remains a barrier to both research and intervention.

Our own research, and that of many other qualitative researchers, highlights the need to spend time in the field establishing rapport and trust with stakeholders and community groups. Qualitative research on food insecurity tends to take a long time. We have found that talking to food aid volunteers can be a useful strategy. They usually have a strong overview of local stressors around food insecurity can often help with recruitment. Added to which, many of the volunteers we have spoken to ended up volunteering after experiencing food insecurity themselves – and then wanted to 'give something back'. Others move between volunteering when they are able to and using food aid services themselves when they are having 'a rough patch'. In practice, the line between service user and service provider is not a clear one. Qualitative research can help capture and deal with the 'messiness' of the food aid landscape. We have found that multiple interviews with the same participant is often necessary to do justice to these. The first interview is typically taken up covering the problems and crises that led to first having to go without food and/or access a food bank. Once this is established, subsequent interviews can focus more on particular research questions, such as the acceptability of certain services or perceptions of local need.

## Unexpected strategies and stories

While the drivers of food insecurity and the hardship it causes are well-trodden in terms of research, exploratory qualitive work is particularly valuable in terms of understanding everyday strategies to cope with food insecurity and its impacts. For example, both money saving and environmental advice highlight the disadvantages of buying bottled water. And yet research from North America shows that those on low incomes are buying and consuming increasing quantities of bottled water (5). If they used tap water instead, this is money that could be spent on other things, especially food. However, for those experiencing chronic uncertainty and food insecurity, buying bottled water makes a lot of sense. If you live in temporary accommodation, shelters, refuges, or houses of multiple occupation (HMO), there can be limited access to kitchen facilities and sometimes even running water. It can be unsafe to wander in to shared kitchen facilities to fetch water and, if you have small children, this can be even more risky or might involve leaving them on their own in a room that does not lock. Having a good supply of bottled water can provide safety, peace of mind, and the capacity to wash (somewhat) without having to risk using a shared bathroom (if there is one). However familiar a researcher is with the topic of food insecurity, lived experience accounts will also offer new perspectives and rationales for behaviours that might, at first glance, seem counter intuitive or ill advised. This type of information is vitally important for informing interventions that are appropriate and acceptable.

## Quantitative data

Quantitative data – measuring the food environment, counting numbers of people accessing food aid or collecting the costs of a comparative basket of goods – has been a substantial focus of research into food insecurity, as seen in previous chapters. Quantitative approaches can generate 'objective' evidence about the local food environments and experiences of those who live, work, or go to school in these areas. The local authorities we work with have found this type of evidence to be easily communicated through tables, graphs and maps, engaging people who can make decisions about priorities. Because there was much emphasis placed on food desert research over the last few decades, this methodology is typically well understood. Further, the data generated through such measurement can be easily replicated for follow-up research over time to identify changes to food environments, costs, or prevalence of food insecurity and related health in the population. The main elements of this approach can demonstrate how the built environment, which impacts upon food access in a given area, may change. We can also explore how costs of food change over time, which in the UK has been a growing concern. One food poverty campaigner, Jack Monroe, has suggested a price index to capture change over time in a set of items that lower-income households would be likely to purchase (6), such as budget range tinned foods and pasta. This approach to price monitoring aligns with the Thrifty Food Plan basket in the US. Whatever the food basket source, the benefit of these data is an ability to monitor costs across an area and, if there is capacity, over time.

## Where is the food?

The sources of data about food resources can be secondary (already available), or primary (collected by the research team for the specific project). The benefits of secondary data are the lower cost, compared to collecting new primary data which typically requires the assistance of staff who have to be taken off other projects and/or employed on the project. To begin a piece of work on food environments in an area, the initial data requirement is a list of retail stores (restaurants, cafes, and fast food or takeaways are often not included as the focus is on food to buy and prepare at home) and other food sources, such as food banks. Retail food establishments will be included in environmental health datasets held by local governments and lists of these are usually available following an email request. The list may include a range of data such as address and opening hours which can provide fuller profile of the retail food environment in terms of temporal accessibility. Thinking about when stores are open compared to when people are able to shop enables us to consider non-standard working patterns like shift work and night work. Other data sources in the UK include the free datasets compiled by Geolytix, which cover supermarket and convenience store retail locations, and the licensed Points of Interest data by Ordnance Survey, which is available for public sector use. Each of these datasets can be mapped using Geographic Information Systems (GIS) to explore the spatial distribution of retail access. More details are provided in Box 5.1.

Once a set of food locations are provided and mapped, the next step is to assess the reliability of the data. Burgoine and Harrison compared local government register data with Points of Interest and found significant disagreement for convenience stores, and, more generally in rural areas (7). The best option would be to undertake some level of ground truthing, where researchers check the accuracy of the data sets in a sample of the data. A recent example from the US demonstrated poor agreement between local government records and a sample of streets visited in person (8), reinforcing the need to quality assess the records provided. We would recommend checking the accuracy of a minimum of 10% of the records (9) and also for a variety of deprivation/poverty classifications by small areas. These could be census tracts in the US or Lower Super Output Areas (LSOA) in England. Researchers should ensure that any ground truthing is completed in a relatively short time period, ideally no more than two weeks. Further, that inaccurate or partially inaccurate records are noted as such. Changes of business name must also be noted, even if the overall category remains the same.

## BOX 5.1

**Mapping the retail environment**

*Resources:*

1. Contact your local council and ask for the food premises register, often held by Environmental Health

2. If public sector, look at Ordnance Survey's Points of Interest dataset: www.ordnancesurvey.co.uk/business-government/tools -support/points-of-interest-support
3. A free resource is the regularly compiled Supermarket Retail Points by Geolytix: https://geolytix.com/blog/supermarket-retail -points-v22/

*Considerations:*

1. Ground truth (visit in person) a sample of 10% of your area. Use a range of localities that differ based on population characteristics such as welfare recipients or BAME populations
2. Complete this ground truthing in a short time period, such as a month
3. If you are using multiple researchers, ensure they are consistently assessing the retail environments against clear criteria: presence/ absence of named store, change in store name, change in use of premises

*Measuring access:*

1. Use free mapping software (QGIS https://qgis.org/en/site/about/ index.html) to measure access to food sources
2. For a starting point, use free postcode location data from Ordnance Survey, Code-Point Open: https://osdatahub.os.uk/ downloads/open/CodePointOpen
3. For the end points, you can use the postcodes of the stores or food aid locations and create a file with just these locations
4. In GIS packages, the typical tool for measuring the distances between one origin point (all postcodes) to the closest destination (postcodes of shops/food aid) is called Distance to Nearest Hub (points) in QGIS or Near in ArcGIS. Run this tool and then take the median value for your small areas, such as LSOAs. The median value can be calculated by exporting the data from the GIS into Microsoft Excel and creating a Pivot Table where data are grouped by LSOA
5. If there is time and capacity, explore the options for public transport to shops and food aid. Where is the nearest bus/metro/underground stop, and how frequent is the service?
6. If time is short, use the E-food desert index for the UK (13) or the Food Access Research Atlas for the US (14). Both include some population demographic characteristics as well

---

***Food basket comparisons: recommendations***

1. Agree a short list of foods that reflect local population preferences. Consider adapting a version of the USDA Thrifty Food Plan

2. Prioritise the diet quality as appropriate: consult a nutritionist for optimal basket of goods or work with target populations to reflect what is most often purchased

3. How to account for missing items which totalling the cost of the basket: take an average cost of the items at other shops from the same chain, that are the same size. For example, if frozen peas are not available in one Sainsbury's local, calculate the price based on all chain smaller-format stores

4. Do not include temporary price reductions or discounted goods (yellow sticker) as this will not represent the usual situation

5. Price the basket at stores in varied levels of socioeconomic deprivation to identify if prices vary by this characteristic

6. Price the basket in large and smaller format stores, including chain stores where possible

---

When planning on a sample of shops to price exemplar baskets of food, ensure that the stores represent a range of options for local residents. We suggest only pricing the baskets at a range of stores and not just the larger chain supermarkets as these can be inaccessible without a car or public transport. For example, in a recent study of a semi-rural area of England we found that many people cannot afford to drive to the nearby large supermarket and there were few or no available buses (10). Our sampling strategy was to price out a basket of goods at all formats of one national chain (here, Tesco) including its large supermarket and small convenience store formats. Where there was no chain store available, we priced the goods at any shop that was present. In some small communities, this was a farm shop where prices were much higher. In areas where there were several stores available, we sampled from a range of the most affordable chain stores, to reflect the known preferences of lower-income households.

A similar basket comparison in a larger city took a two-stage sampling approach for market basket comparison. First, the LSOAs were classified using the most recent Index of Multiple Deprivation (2015) and an equal sample of LSOAs was selected from each deprivation quintile (categorising all LSOAs into five equal sized groups) as classified for the city, not using the national quintiles of deprivation. Then, we used the local government's register of retail food stores to identify the locations of chain and non-chain supermarkets and convenience stores across the city. Ideally a separate ground truthing exercise would be undertaken. However, there were limited resources so this occurred only as part of the market basket pricing. In each selected LSOA at least one supermarket (if available) and one convenience store were selected for the pricing.

Food basket comparisons can take into account the types of foods people purchase regularly, such as Monroe's proposed basket, or can also factor-in the healthiness of food available. In one recent example we co-developed a basket of 20 items with people accessing support for food, based on items they regularly purchased (10). This basket included toothpaste, toilet roll and nappies/diapers and sanitary items that are regularly requested at food banks. While not all items are food, it reflected the reality of what people need to spend food budgets on. Work completed in London used a basket developed with nutrition as a priority, with a more extensive list of food items (11).

## Adding place-based resources and population characteristics

A focus on the positive characteristics and assets of areas is key to a place-based approach. What opportunities are available to support people who may need help with food and other necessities? If we revisit the conceptual framework from Chapter 4, we are reminded to consider the context people live within, and to think about the range of pressures that influence food insecurity. Additional assets, beyond support with food and income, include those which support mental and physical health more broadly. We would suggest looking at what is available in terms of access to healthcare through formal channels as well as charities that support people who have mental ill health, such as Mind. Having more support in managing ill health, mental or physical, can help to address food insecurity in the longer term. Including details of available social prescribers, who work in collaboration with GPs to signpost people to other services, is a useful step. Talking directly to these prescribers will give more information about the range of resources where they act as referring agents.

Income is at the root of many of the national drivers and local stressors of food insecurity. However, income is influenced by other considerations around (secure) housing and employment, access to transportation, skills and training/education and affordable childcare. In the next section, the people/populations at the core of this research are brought into the data collection process, then we look at local assets.

**Where are the people?**

Now that we have made a start with collating food environment data and identifying the resources in an area, we think about the key populations who experience food insecurity and why. In smaller scale research this can be accomplished by talking with food aid organisations to find out who tends to access support. It warrants repeating, though, that relatively few people experiencing some level of food insecurity will ask for assistance. Estimates suggest that only between 20 and 50% of people who are food insecure seek help (12, 13). In the geographic area of focus, the next step is to identify if there are frequent characteristics of households using food aid, such as those with very young children or older adults living alone. These details can be collected at the same time you are enquiring about the opening hours and referral system in place to access their services.

If there is not sufficient capacity to collect this data through interviews, you could use a risk measure for food insecurity in local areas. In England there are direct (14) or indirect (15) measures. The direct measure is at a coarser scale of local authority districts (similar to a US county), while the indirect risk measure is for neighbourhoods. In our studies, we use as a starting point the indirect measure of household food insecurity risk in small areas (LSOAs), available to download from www. mylocalmap.org .uk (Figure 5.1). This measure was informed by a scoping literature review and qualitative interviews with stakeholder across the South of England. Four variables are included, all as a percentage of the local population: benefits claimants, low-income households that are either single adults or with dependent children, people with no educational qualifications, and people experiencing mental health problems. The direct measure uses a statistical model to predict how many people experience food insecurity in local authorities based on a survey from the Food Foundation (14).

Another concern is the poverty premium, where people on lower incomes tend to face higher unavoidable living costs such as food (as described in Chapter 2) and energy, as they may have only prepayment meters rather than a pay monthly tariff for their household energy supply. The need to pay monthly rather than annually for other big costs, such as insurance, can also add more to total costs. The area someone lives in can influence the cost of home and car insurance, with premiums up to £300 more in areas classified as most deprived (top 20%) in the Index of Multiple Deprivation. Finally, the need to rely on higher-interest credit when money is very short can cost much more over time than lower interest credit cards. These direct costs are in addition to already lower incomes, thereby amplifying income inequality (16).

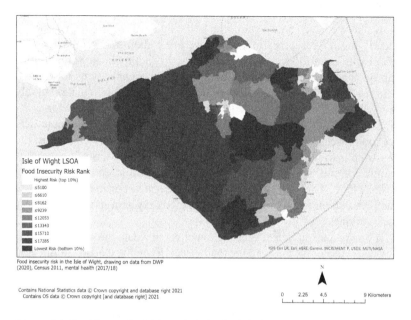

Isle of Wight LSOA
Food Insecurity Risk Rank
Highest Risk (top 10%)
≤5100
≤6610
≤8162
≤9239
≤12053
≤13343
≤15710
≤17285
Lowest Risk (bottom 10%)

Food insecurity risk in the Isle of Wight, drawing on data from DWP
(2020), Census 2011, mental health (2017/18)

Contains National Statistics data © Crown copyright and database right 2021
Contains OS data © Crown copyright [and database right] 2021

0    2.25    4.5              9 Kilometers

*Figure 5.1*  Food Insecurity Risk on the Isle of Wight, in Lower Super Output Areas.
Highest risk is shown as lightest.

Food environments are not only about retail food, as we noted in 2019
they should also encompass the food aid options in a locality (17). There is
rarely a list of food aid sources readily available, and this has been a source
of frustration from our partners when developing Food Poverty Action Plans.
In some of our research we have used qualitative interviews with stakeholders to find out: what food aid is available in a given area, when it is available,
and to whom (access) (10). Access to food aid, via food banks and similar, is
not a straightforward process. Referral mechanisms are usually in place and
food aid outlets have limited opening hours, sometimes being open for only
a few hours once or twice a week. In Box 5.2 we set out a process for finding out more information about the support offered in localities to those who
are food insecure. This focuses entirely on food aid rather than the upstream
interventions of welfare advice services such as Citizen's Advice, who help
people with financial concerns. We also include a summary of the dominant
models of food aid and support currently operating in the UK.

**BOX 5.2**

**Mapping the food aid environment**

*Community food intervention models*

When mapping out the assets in a community as part of any study, these are some frequent intervention types you may see. The names and terms can differ, which is where the qualitative work will support your resource finding mission. We include web links for national organisations in the UK to provide a starting point as many will list what is available in different areas by searching from city names or postcodes. In all of the following examples the hours of operation are often limited.

**Community Fridge:** (see www.hubbub.org.uk/the-community -fridge): typically free for anyone to come and collect what is needed, no referral required. Food may be contributed by other people in the community, surplus food from commercial sources. There tends to a focus on fresh food, people choose what they want to take home. Some do ask for a donation, e.g., https://midsurreycommunityfridges.co.uk/

**Community Pantry:** (see www.yourlocalpantry.co.uk/): a membership food shop where items (both fresh produce and ambient, longer shelf life) are greatly discounted, usually no referral is needed to join but they are often restricted to set geographic areas. Members chose a set number of items for a price.

**Community/Mobile Larder:** (see https://basicsbank.org.uk/new -mobile-larder/): a mobile version of the community pantry, designed to reach more remote areas where there is not capacity for an established or stationary location. As with a pantry there is a minimal charge for a bag of ambient goods and fresh produce, but often there is not a choice of goods provided.

**Food Banks:** (Trussell Trust www.trusselltrust.org/ and IFAN https://www.foodaidnetwork.org.uk/): the most established type of food aid in the UK, usually a referral is required for people to be given food for 3–5 days, limited/no choice of food. Mostly ambient items unless there is local capacity to store fresh produce or chilled/frozen foods. Food is provided by donation from the public or through surplus food distribution organisations.

**Social Supermarket:** (see www.companyshopgroup.co.uk/community-shop-our-social-enterprise): similar to a community pantry, but operates like a supermarket in that people are able to use their membership to visit the store and choose what they want to buy. The main sources of food are mislabelled or other surplus food items, and profits can be used to support additional initiatives to help members with skills, cooking, and training.

**Community Café:** (see www.foodcycle.org.uk/): a pay as you can café where often food and labour is donated, with food from surplus sources. No referral required.

**Community Gardens:** (see www.rhs.org.uk/get-involved/community-gardening): community or charity run gardens where food is shared out among volunteers or local residents, sometimes produce is made available via a community fridge.

*Finding resources*

1. Web searches for food banks, community fridges, food pantries and other terms listed above
2. Participatory mapping with community members – ask different groups to share their knowledge of local opportunities through schools, places of worship, any community groups.
3. Facebook/online groups for local areas where such services are often shared
4. Contact schools, places of worship and community centres to ask if they provide food to families
5. Interviews with local stakeholders and residents to see where they signpost or access food

*Adding detail*

1. Once the sites are identified, find out the referral method (self-referral, external party referral)
2. Collect opening hours and any seasonal changes
3. Call to check they are still operating and accepting new clients
4. Note how often clients can access the resource: unlimited, once per week, three or six times a year

## Tensions within food aid and surplus food redistribution

As set out in previous chapters, the issues of food waste and food insecurity have become regrettably intertwined, with food waste sometimes posited as a straightforward response to food insecurity via the redistribution of surplus food. Practical work to address food insecurity at the local level necessitates working with food waste and food surplus charities, which do important work and campaigning. The food insecurity/food waste coupling remains fraught with tensions.

In the US, Andrew Fisher systematically describes the evolution of food aid structures that are politically supported, preventing investment in upstream interventions to address household food insecurity (18). This historical approach to food aid, redistribution of surplus food and institutionalisation of charitable food aid instead of state aid, has been explored extensively by Janet Poppendieck (19, 20). The impact of ongoing charitable sector intervention has somewhat taken pressure off governments to intervene. This reliance on third sector support creates an additional level of precarity for food insecure households as access to food aid may be mediated by gatekeepers (21) and limited by volunteer resources. The use of food banks and other food aid as the primary response to food insecurity in the UK has been identified by Williams and colleagues as an 'excuse' for the state not to intervene more systematically (22).

In the UK, corporate social responsibility (CSR) is heavily implicated in responses to food insecurity and its inherent framing as a matter for charity, rather than a human right. Food deserts rhetoric and policy created justifications for opening more supermarkets. After all, large chains opening stores in deprived areas could be framed as a way of directly resolving food deserts. For example, Tesco to opened a megastore in a deprived food desert in Seacroft, Leeds (23). Further, corporate social responsibility in the form of reducing food waste enables and justifies large retailers to make vast donations of surplus food to charities such as FareShare. This food is then redistributed to food banks and other food aid settings, while the organisations who provide this food may benefit by writing off the food as a donation (or similar – see https://fareshare.org.uk/giving-food/).

Midgely offers a useful critique of the government approach to surplus food, as outlined in the Food Industry Sustainability Strategy published by the Department for Environment, Food and Rural Affairs (DEFRA) in 2006. Surplus food was positioned as *a possible public health benefit*, precisely because it could be (re)distributed by charities to those on lower incomes (24). Again, it is charities, and not the state, who are integral (and therefore responsible?) for feeding hungry households. This system raises difficult questions that are not easily answered nor resolved. Is the surplus food provided by FareShare always what is needed or wanted by individuals who are at the receiving end of this charity? What happens 'waste' food that is classified as such but never finds its way to the households who need it? The supermarkets have benefited from its classification as a food waste reduction, but without the intended recipients necessarily benefitting from it.

Some small charities comment on having to get rid of the food themselves, creating another burden for their limited resources.

## Ladders of support (what does the food aid environment look like?)

Recently there has been a proliferation of alternative formats of food aid in the UK, including community fridges, food pantries, mobile larders, and online resources for sharing food such as Olio and Too Good to Go (see Box 5.2). Each of these services is free or charges very little for people who want or need food. These services can also work to reduce waste as much of the fresh produce especially would be at risk of not being consumed if not diverted to these outlets. The distributing of food, in these cases, is framed as helping to reduce food waste rather than as food aid or poverty relief. Despite the limitations and tensions around surplus food as a 'solution' to food insecurity, the fact remains that it does help provide relief and, therefore, the services that distribute it are assets that need to be mapped and understood. However, it can be challenging to keep track of the food aid assets at any scale, and especially locally. By their very nature, third sector and community-led services of this kind have a high turnover, often depend on donated space and volunteer labour, and the locations of outlets may change.

We have observed efforts to map both the retail food environment and the range of food aid organisations across local areas across England. Blake's framework for thinking about community food security interventions, food ladders (25) is outlined in Chapter 4. In essence, the model describes 'rungs' of a ladder to allow varied levels of support for people to help them move/climb out of food insecurity. This progresses from emergency provision such as food banks at the bottom rung, moving to capacity building such as food pantries that include some choice and agency for clients. The final rung is 'self-organised community change' with a focus on local social enterprise. These ladders can be developed for specific local areas, to map out what is present and what is needed, and can support strategic planning at the local level – especially for Food Poverty Action Plans (FPAPs).

In our work we often focus on the bottom two rungs of this ladder where resources are targeted at people in acute and/or chronic food insecurity. Part of the second rung is around longer-term solutions such as welfare maximisation to improve income and support with cooking and budgeting to help people make their money and food last longer and go further. Just as there are national organisations for food banks (Independent Food Aid Network and the Trussell Trust) there is now one for food pantries, Your Local Pantry (www.yourlocalpantry.co.uk/), which operates membership-only subsidised food stores in local communities. Users (members) pay a small amount to access the shop and, unlike food banks, no referral is required.

There are cooking clubs (see for example, Good Grub Club www.stmary-sandover.org/whatson/ggc) that usually target families during school holidays to help reduce holiday hunger (where children experience food insecurity during breaks in school without access to free school meals). The benefit of these clubs includes building skills in cooking for families and engaging children and parents together to cook and eat different foods. The incorporation of skills as well as free food during, and sometimes in take-home bags after the sessions, addresses both food security and capacity building at the household level.

Community gardens are now a feature in many US cities (www.communitygarden.org/) and increasingly in the UK too. There are a range of variations of this model, from people growing food fully collectively to smaller individual plots, like allotments. The food can be shared among members or more widely among the community. In the UK, it is growing evermore difficult to get an allotment. The process for obtaining one is increasingly competitive and it is not uncommon to be placed on a waiting list for years. This is extremely problematic because growing food *is* a sustainable and longer-term solution to chronic food insecurity. It is also one that requires those involved to have time available to engage with growing, and access to a garden. Ideally there would be a network in place to ensure any produce that can be shared more widely is delivered to a community fridge or pantry; there are examples of this practice in England, in Bournemouth.[1]

## Exploring local food insecurity stressors

The drivers of food insecurity are upstream, or structural, factors that negatively impact on household income and the cost of living. Local stressors are more downstream barriers such as the location and opening hours of services. Some drivers are indirect and personal, such as poor mental health. The challenge is to bring together data that can adequately capture the layers of local stressors alongside the local assets and facilitators that can be deployed to mitigate them. The overall aim is to identify effective leverage points for intervention.

We recommend that researchers use a similar process to identify local stressors in communities to those steps they would apply to mapping the food aid environment. Here, we suggest using qualitative interviews as a first phase to find out what the perceived barriers to food security are for people living in the area. Local benefits advisors, social prescribers or GPs (family doctors), food aid providers, and residents accessing these services are best placed to share with you their reflections and experience. During these interviews you can also find out what their ideal solutions to food insecurity would be, thus compiling context-relevant and realistic potential approaches and ideas for interventions (10) and resource prioritisation. If interviews or focus groups are not feasible, then one alternative we used recently was a survey collected at sites of food aid which included open-ended questions to capture the drivers of food insecurity (Ibid).

The urban/rural distinction can also have an influential role in food security, as there tend to be more assets and facilitators of food security in more populated areas. In England there is acknowledged locational disadvantages to living in more rural areas, where private transportation may be needed to access health care, well paid employment and educational opportunities that will improve earning ability (26). In some rural areas the level of housing benefit does not reflect the cost of private rented accommodation and there is limited stock of social housing (10). These living costs need to be acknowledged in any research on food security, as they require limited household budgets to stretch further, reducing money available for food.

The next issue facing more isolated locations is access to food aid. As we outlined in Chapter 4, what support is available may not be physically accessible by public transport and often has short opening hours, with some services only available for a few hours each week. This was the case in rural England, where mobile food larders were considered a lifeline by many clients, but are only available in their areas two hours, once a week. The other issue noted with regards to food aid in more rural areas is that 'everyone knows who you are', which causes some people not to seek support when they need it for fear of being recognised (10, 22).

Further data collection on local stressors should include unavoidable living costs such as private rented housing, availability of social housing, and the numbers of prepayment electricity meters in households within small areas. All of this can be benchmarked or compared to the regional or national data to see the magnitude of difference. These data will provide some indication of the living costs within an area. Then, access to opportunities to increase income can be collected by mapping public transport frequency and cost to areas of higher employment and further/higher education.

All the proposed data collection activities above can be informed and refined based on the qualitative interviews with stakeholders and clients, which will provide vital context and may even identify local stressors that we have yet to encounter. We have heard anecdotal accounts of the presence of army barracks, care homes, traveller sites, food processing plants, and even prisons presenting challenges for local food security. These warrant further attention from researchers.

Once the main points of interest are identified, there are a wealth of online resources in addition to those already noted for data about people and areas. A key word search on https://data.gov.uk/ will identify open data that can be included in local mapping. Additional datasets such as internet user classifications are available from the Consumer Data Research Centre (www.cdrc.ac.uk/). For population health data, there are resources at coarser geographies (local districts) at https://fingertips.phe.org.uk/ for England, https://phw.nhs.wales/data/ for Wales, the Scottish Public Health Observatory (www.scotpho.org.uk/) and the Public Health Agency of Northern Ireland (www.publichealth.hscni.net/directorates/operations/statistics).

## The challenges of place-based research

One of the major challenges facing researchers looking at local-level food insecurity is that of churn and uncertainty. Funding for food insecurity interventions in the charity sector is often precarious and short term. Food banks and food pantries 'pop up' in areas and then can disappear after a few months. Charities and community groups often struggle to source and maintain adequate funding for their services (27). It is a constant challenge for those providing services and for those working in local authority public health teams, who need to keep track of the ever-changing food aid landscape. This is compounded by the fact that statutory funding for local authority teams to work on addressing food insecurity is also often short term and precarious. Fixed-term posts for six or 12 months to lead a needs assessment or set up Food Poverty Action Plans are not uncommon. The post holder will do important, valuable work and make a wealth of local contacts. But if their contract cannot be renewed that information can be lost when they move on to another post or placement. For researchers applying for external funding this can be especially difficult. The person you work with when drafting a funding bid may well have moved on by the time you submit the bid and might have been replaced a number of times by time the research itself gets underway. New people in post may not have the time or inclination to engage with researchers in the way their predecessor(s) have and the whole process can end up resetting. We have found that working with local groups like Healthwatch (www.healthwatch.co.uk/what-we-do) can be a useful way of offsetting this churn. They maintain a steady presence in communities that food aid organisations, local authority employees, and fixed-term funded academic researchers are not always able to.

## Political alignments and barriers

As we have argued at length, (food) poverty is a political issue. Researching and addressing food insecurity at the local level can become entangled with local politics. When working on food poverty action plans in various local authorities, we have found that Labour-leaning and

Conservative-leaning boroughs and local Councillors can take very different stances on the issue. Some ambitious local politicians might want to champion food insecurity issues and food banks prior to being elected, and then become significantly less engaged once the pressures of their post take hold. There is no appetite for announcing a Food Poverty Action Plan or needs assessment around local election time, as it can be seen as a public declaration of failure to tackle poverty on the part of the incumbent party of the candidate. Even the name *Food Poverty Action Plan* has proved unpalatable in some localities, who would rather not have the word 'poverty' in the title of anything they do.

## Measuring impact

Impact measurement of food aid or support is not the top priority, understandably, of most interventions like food pantries or food banks. Their primary goal is to support people experiencing food insecurity either immediately, in the case of food banks, or longer term in the examples of social supermarkets and community hubs. The interventions may at times need to collect data that allows them to demonstrate how much their support has helped people who are food insecure. This impact measurement can be a means to an end for further funding (28), as an evidence base is required before local councils or external funding bodies will invest in community-based organisations. Whoever is investing in these services will want an indication of 'success'. Ideally, this would be the situation where no extra help is required, though realistically success may be moving households from the bottom rung (food banks) to a higher agency rung of the food ladder like a social supermarket, or a normal retail outlet. In our conversations with those providing food aid, their aim is to support this transition.

Measuring impact of any intervention is challenging, as described in Chapter 4. We have recently started a few projects where data on the impact of interventions will be collected using a mixed methods approach. In order to understand the impact on service users, or 'clients' we use interviews with clients of food aid services to find out if and how their food security changed as a result of using the intervention. For practical reasons, including time constraints and the challenges of recruitment, this is typically a relatively small sample. We recommend offering a supermarket voucher or similar as a gesture of appreciation to those that agree to be interviewed. We also ask more clients to fill in a short survey at their first visit to or interaction with the intervention (where possible), which captures their food security situation, using the USDA food security questions, modified to reflect the experience of the previous 30 days (29). We use a validated measure of wellbeing (30) to understand their current mental wellbeing and ask them to answer questions about diet quality, such as the portions of fruit and vegetables. Finally, the survey asks about their ability to make the best use of food available to them and includes questions about what would help them in terms of food security. The survey can be repeated regularly across a year, to see if any of the answers about these outcomes change. Where we cannot collect the data at first point of contact with the intervention, we may ask the questions retrospectively at a later date.

To understand the perspective of the service providers, we interview representatives from the food aid groups to ask about the difficulties they experience in the day-to-day running of their services and what their plans are for the immediate and longer term. This forms part of a process evaluation. We will also interview local government colleagues who oversee the funding allocations for these activities to understand what they observe about the food aid groups and impact on clients. Has it changed any population-level aid seeking, such as requests for food and fuel vouchers? All of this activity addresses the WHO recommendation to measure impact (31).

## Strategies for collaboration and dissemination

A strategy for success in area-based research is to maintain communication with your contacts in the aligned groups, such as food banks and local government teams. Provide updates on the research progression and if this work is completed as part of a project for an educational qualification, agree what will be shared with any external partners at the end of the process.

A long document is not the most useful output for people who need to make a case to local planners for priority funding, for example. Ask what would work well for your partners, such as a short policy briefing document (no more than two pages), set of slides or a short presentation to an audience. We find that alternative formats such as short project videos can also increase impact from research or providing a launch event of a larger report. For more advice on collaboratively devising research projects on food inequality, please see Sustain's Food Power group and their guide to Food Poverty Action Plans, with links to examples (www.sustainweb.org /foodpower/).

## Summary

Our applied research framework aims to understand the extent and causes of household food insecurity in specific communities. It is a process that can be followed to study food insecurity in localities and enables a holistic understanding of 1) where food access limiting people's diets and 2) what can be done to improve access. The framework can be adapted to explore predominantly financial barriers to food as well as the scenarios where accessibility is limited by mobility, distance, or social isolation. We encourage the mapping of both positive and negative aspects of the setting for research, building on research on asset-based mapping (32) and salutogenic environments (environments which promote good health), similar to the previously discussed obesogenic environments (33).

## Note

1  See www.facebook.com/TOWNSENDCOMMUNITYFRIDGE

## References

1.  Pourmotabbed A, Moradi S, Babaei A, Ghavami A, Mohammadi H, Jalili C, et al. Food insecurity and mental health: a systematic review and meta-analysis. *Public Health Nutrition.* 2020;23(10):1778–90.
2.  Moraes C, McEachern MG, Gibbons A, Scullion L. Understanding lived experiences of food insecurity through a paraliminality lens. *Sociology.* 2021;55(6):1169–90.
3.  Pearson B, Guerlain M, Shaw S. *Telling stories and shaping solutions: A toolkit for empowering people who have lived experience of food poverty.* Sustain, 2020.
4.  McIntosh I, Wright S. Exploring what the notion of 'lived experience' offers for social policy analysis. *Journal of Social Policy.* 2019;48(3):449–67.
5.  Family L, Zheng G, Cabezas M, Cloud J, Hsu S, Rubin E, et al. *The Journal of the American Dental Association.* 2019;150(6):503–13.
6.  Monroe J. We're pricing the poor out of food in the UK: that's why I'm launching my own price index. *The Guardian.* 2022 22 January.
7.  Burgoine T, Harrison F. Comparing the accuracy of two secondary food environment data sources in the UK across socio-economic and urban/rural divides. *International Journal of Health Geographics.* 2013;12(1):2.
8.  Lucan SC, Maroko AR, Abrams C, Rodriguez N, Patel AN, Gjonbalaj I, et al. Government data v. ground observation for food-environment assessment: Businesses missed and misreported by city and state inspection records. *Public Health Nutrition.* 2020;23(8):1414–27.
9.  Rossen LM, Pollack KM, Curriero FC. Verification of retail food outlet location data from a local health department using ground-truthing and remote-sensing technology: Assessing differences by neighborhood characteristics. *Health & Place.* 2012;18(5):956–62.
10.  Smith DM, Paddon L, Group CoLS. *Cost of living in the new forest.* University of Southampton, Citizens Advice New Forest; 2021.
11.  Nzuza N, Duval D. *Royal borough of Greenwich food poverty needs assessment.* Royal Borough of Greenwich; 2016.

12. Tarasuk V, Fafard St-Germain A-A, Loopstra R. The relationship between food banks and food insecurity: insights from Canada. *VOLUNTAS: International Journal of Voluntary and Nonprofit Organizations*. 2020;31(5):841–52.

13. The Food Foundation. *The impact of Covid-19 on household food security*. The Food Foundation; 2021.

14. Moretti A, Whitworth A, Blake M. *UK local food insecurity methods briefing*. University of Sheffield; 2021.

15. University of Southampton, Smith D. *Local area data and mapping*. 2021 Available from: https://www.mylocalmap.org.uk/iaahealth/.

16. Davies S, Trend L. *The poverty premium: a customer perspective*. University of Bristol; 2020.

17. Thompson C, Smith D, Cummins S. Food banking and emergency food aid: expanding the definition of local food environments and systems. *International Journal of Behavioral Nutrition and Physical Activity*. 2019;16(1):2.

18. Fisher A. *Big hunger: the unholy alliance between corporate America and anti-hunger groups*. The MIT Press; 2017.

19. Poppendieck J. Hunger in America: typification and response. in D Maurer and J Sobal (Eds) *Eating Agendas: Food and Nutrition as Social Problems*. 1995:11–34.

20. Poppendieck J. *Sweet charity?: Emergency food and the end of entitlement*. Penguin; 1999.

21. Thompson C, Smith D, Cummins S. Understanding the health and wellbeing challenges of the food banking system: A qualitative study of food bank users, providers and referrers in London. *Social Science & Medicine*. 2018;211:95–101.

22. Williams A, Cloke P, May J, Goodwin M. Contested space: the contradictory political dynamics of food banking in the UK. *Environment and Planning A*. 2016;48(11):2291–316.

23. Wrigley N, Warm D, Margetts B. Deprivation, diet, and food-retail access: findings from the leeds 'food deserts' study. *Environment and Planning A*. 2003;35(1):151–88.

24. Midgley JL. The logics of surplus food redistribution. *Journal of Environmental Planning and Management*. 2014;57(12):1872–92.

25. Blake M. *Food ladders: a multi-scaled approach to everyday food security and community resilience*. University of Sheffield, ESTC, MRC, N8 AgriFood Programme; 2019.

26. Rural Services Network. *Rural vulnerability and disadvantage statement 2020*. Rural England. 2020.

27. Thompson C, Smith S, Cummins S. Understanding the health and wellbeing challenges of the food banking system: A qualitative study of food bank users, providers and referrers in London. *Social Science & Medicine*. 2018;211:95–101.

28. Thomson H. A dose of realism for healthy urban policy: lessons from area-based initiatives in the UK. *Journal of Epidemiology and Community Health*. 2008;62(10):932–6.

29. United States Department of Agriculture Economic Research Service. *Food security in the US survey tools*. 2021 Available from: https://www.ers .usda.gov/topics/food-nutrition-assistance/food-security-in-the-u-s/survey-tools/.

30. Tennant R, Hiller, L., Fishwick, R., Platt, S., Joseph, S., Weich, S., ... & Stewart-Brown, S. The Warwick-Edinburgh mental well-being scale (WEMWBS): Development and UK validation. 2007. *Health and Quality of Life Outcomes*. 2007;5:63.

31. World Health Organization. *Closing the gap in a generation: health equity through action on the social determinants of health - Final report of the commission on social determinants of health*. World Health Organization; 2008.

32. Soma T, Shulman T, Li B, Bulkan J, Curtis M. Food assets for whom? Community perspectives on food asset mapping in Canada. *Journal of Urbanism: International Research on Placemaking and Urban Sustainability*. 2021:1–18. doi:10.1080/17549175.2021.1918750.

33. Egger G, Swinburn B. An "ecological" approach to the obesity pandemic. *BMJ*. 1997;315(7106):477–80.

# 6  The changing landscape of food insecurity research

## Key themes and trends in food insecurity research

We set out to provide an overview and guide for those interested in, or tasked with, assessing food insecurity in its various forms in local areas. We are not aware of any existing summaries of essential concepts aligned with food insecurity at the local level or advice on how to undertake research at this scale. We wanted to provide support for people who are working to understand the extent of food insecurity in their localities.

Our conceptual framework is devised as two sets of data considerations: (i) local food insecurity stressors and (ii) resources and facilitators for mitigating food insecurity. In terms of method, we recommend a combination of using available quantitative data on retail or food aid locations and population characteristics with supporting details and asset identification from qualitative methods. This approach is underpinned by four main considerations and themes:

**National vs local measurement** is a necessary starting point for local teams, as it gives an indication of how severe food insecurity might be in the community. Measurement can be primary data collection or using a secondary measure such as those available in both the US and the UK, described in chapter 2, where the data need to be spatially precise. A higher-level (national) monitoring process from representative surveys is ongoing in both countries. However, the situation in the UK is that these data (from the Family Resource Survey) should *not* be used to indicate local geographic patterns in food insecurity as they cannot be mapped below the level of the nine regions of the UK.

**Local stressors** are context-specific, or place-based, factors that exacerbate income inequality and resulting food insecurity. Collecting information about what people experience that makes it more difficult to have a healthy diet will identity what changes could be made in local areas, such as providing a regular free bus to a larger supermarket where prices

DOI: 10.4324/9781003184560-6

are lower. Essentially, local stressors invariably relate to access to and/or quality of the social determinants of health. This can be a useful starting point when asking local residents and organisations about what makes life difficult and what could make it easier. Education, transport, work opportunities, problems with benefits and housing are all valid areas for investigation. When the local research is conducted in collaboration with organisations who have the power to adapt policy or resources that support food security, there can be positive change to mitigate the impacts of low incomes.

**Asset mapping** helps to identify facilitators of food security, both locally and more broadly in the country. The term asset mapping is used, in practice, to describe a range of approaches. In some instances this might simply be a list of organisations and their locations. The more detailed the 'mapping' (including information on things like opening times, eligibility criteria, referral pathways, and partner organisations) the more useful the exercise. There are standard methods around mapping and measuring the (retail) food environment and we extend this to include the food aid environment in its evolving formats: food banks, pantries, community fridges and gardens to name a few. Research should also include the indirect support options of welfare advice and social prescribers who signpost people to direct aid and recommend steps to income maximisation through benefits. Further assets include the local infrastructure of healthcare and charities which help those with poorer physical and mental health.

**Understanding the limits of the food aid system** is vital to build a complete picture of local assets, capacity, and challenges. The application of concepts such as food ladders will help to structure research into what components of the food aid system are in place in communities. There is a clear postcode lottery situation with food aid, where geographic location can determine access to some services. The food used to support most interventions is donated or surplus food and may lack the nutritional quality needed for people to maintain a good diet (and by extension, health). Food banks themselves also struggle with food waste. Not all of the food they process can or should be given to clients or may even be rejected by them. There is an ongoing level of churn in food aid in terms of personnel and services, which was worsened by the pandemic. This leads to a loss of institutional knowledge that ultimately influences the delivery of these services. Understanding and recognising the pressures faced by food aid can help avoid an uncritical 'handing off' of responsibility from other services, via referral or signposting. Referral to food aid does not mean that the client's problem has been solved or their case closed.

## Towards a community geography model?

An explicitly geographical approach to local-level and place-based research may help to address some of the challenges associated with staffing and funding churn across the third sector, local government, and academic research sectors. Community geography is a pragmatic approach, originating from and established in North America. It is enacted by local coalitions of academics, policy-makers, residents, and sometimes activists (1). These networks of local actors focus on work which enables under-resourced communities to better address community social and development challenges (2). The longer-term and more stable ties to partners and communities outside of the academy that this approach entails can also help avoid and remedy some of the recruitment and ethical challenges that researchers encounter in prevailing systems of research (3). A system of food poverty networks and alliances already exists in the UK (www.sustainweb.org/foodpower/map/). Typically, it is these networks that support and deliver food poverty action plans. They are recent incarnations of long-established civil society and non-state organisations that have been contributing to public health for centuries (4). There are, of course, already academic departments throughout the country that have long been actively working in and with local communities to support them. These local systems of collaboration evolve over time and are responsive to local needs and pressures.

A widespread community geography approach would entail much greater involvement and support of academic geographers, geography departments, and representatives from other academic disciplines, in these systems. Geography, and especially health geography, academics have a long-standing interest in these issues and can support research. While some academics may come and go, the departments remain stable and can be a consistent presence and resource for communities. There is also a steady supply of students every year who have to undertake a research project as part of their studies who could contribute to understanding the local insecurity landscape, in return they gain valuable experience of applied research that could shape their future careers and professional research agendas. Eminent geographer, Danny Dorling, has challenged British and American academics working within the discipline to find ways to re-examine their writing and research priorities in light of stark and widening inequalities (5). A greater involvement – in terms of consistency and longevity – in local efforts to understand and address food insecurity is an excellent way to do this.

## Concluding thoughts

We see some policy moving in positive directions in the UK. The effort to now collect data on household food insecurity creates opportunities to monitor, and therefore challenge, widening inequality (6). In Scotland, progress on the right to food movement can be seen in the Good Food Nation bill, which would support a more sustainable and equitable food system (7). The 2020 pandemic plunged people into hardship, sometimes for the first time in their lives. People who had never had to claim benefits or use food banks found themselves interacting with a system and a set of challenges they were shocked by and unprepared for. Have these collective experiences provided an increased insight and empathy into what it is like to not have free choice with regards to food? There was certainly an uplift in people coming together to help each other in communities during this pandemic. We became aware that our food supply in the UK is heavily reliant on imports and, as a result, there is more interest in community food models to increase environmental sustainability. We hope that this local awareness of how precarious our just-in-time food system can be will serve to galvanize support for local initiatives.

The ability for individuals and households to maintain a healthy diet without resorting to emergency food aid should be a modest goal for any government, and in wealthier counties food insecurity needs to be further up the policy agenda. The UK has been identified as failing to support those in need by the UN rapporteur on extreme poverty. Food insecurity is one such measure of extreme poverty and requires urgent action. As we have described already food is a known social determinant of health that can be conceptualised as basic human right (8). The UK and other wealthy nations are facing a proliferation of non-communicable diseases linked to poor quality diet, often driven by economic concerns at the household level. We remain hopeful that national policy will move forward to tackle pervasive poverty in all its forms, including food insecurity.

## References

1. Shannon J, Hankins KB, Shelton T, Bosse AJ, Scott D, Block D, et al. Community geography: toward a disciplinary framework. *Progress in Human Geography*. 2020;45(5):1147–1168.
2. Robinson JA, Block D, Rees A. Community geography: addressing barriers in public participation GIS. *Cartographic Journal*. 2017;54(1):5–13.
3. Barrett E, Bosse AJ. Community geography for precarious researchers: examining the intricacies of mutually beneficial and co-produced knowledge. *GeoJournal*. 2021. https://link.springer.com/article/10.1007/s10708-020-10358-2.
4. World Health Organization. *Strategic alliances: The role of civil society in health. Civil society initiative.* External Relations and Governing Bodies; 2001. Contract No.: Discussion Paper No. 1. CSI/2001/DP1.

5.  Dorling D. Income inequality in the UK: Comparisons with five large Western European countries and the USA. *Applied Geography*. 2015;61:24–34.

6.  Department for Environment Food and Rural Affairs. *United Kingdom Food Security Report 2021*. Department for Environment Food and Rural Affairs; 2021.

7.  The Scottish Parliament. *Good food nation (Scotland) bill*. 2021 Available from: https://www.parliament.scot/bills-and-laws/bills/good-food-nation -scotland-bill.

8.  Dowler EA, O'Connor D. Rights-based approaches to addressing food poverty and food insecurity in Ireland and UK. *Social Science & Medicine (1982)*. 2012;74(1):44–51.

# Index

Note: Page numbers in *italics* indicate figures, **bold** indicate tables in the text, and references following "n" refer notes

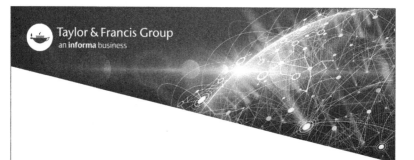

Printed in the United States
by Baker & Taylor Publisher Services